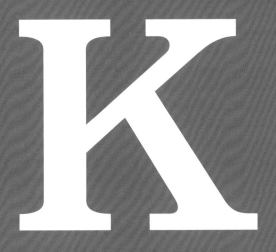

K

42 seasons
FIVE championships
ONE unmatched legacy

The News&Observer   The Charlotte Observer   The Herald·Sun

Credits

BOOK EDITOR

Matt L. Stephens

PHOTO EDITOR

Scott Sharpe

SPORTS EDITOR

Matt L. Stephens

CONTRIBUTING WRITERS

Chip Alexander, Ned Barnett, Andrew Carter,
Luke DeCock, Dane Huffman, Laura Keeley,
Barry Svrluga, Joe Tiede, Ken Tysiac, Steve Wiseman

Published by Pediment Publishing, a division of
The Pediment Group, Inc. • www.pediment.com
Printed in Canada.

This book is an unofficial account of Duke
University basketball coach Mike Krzyzewski's
career and is not endorsed by Duke University or
the National Collegiate Athletic Association.

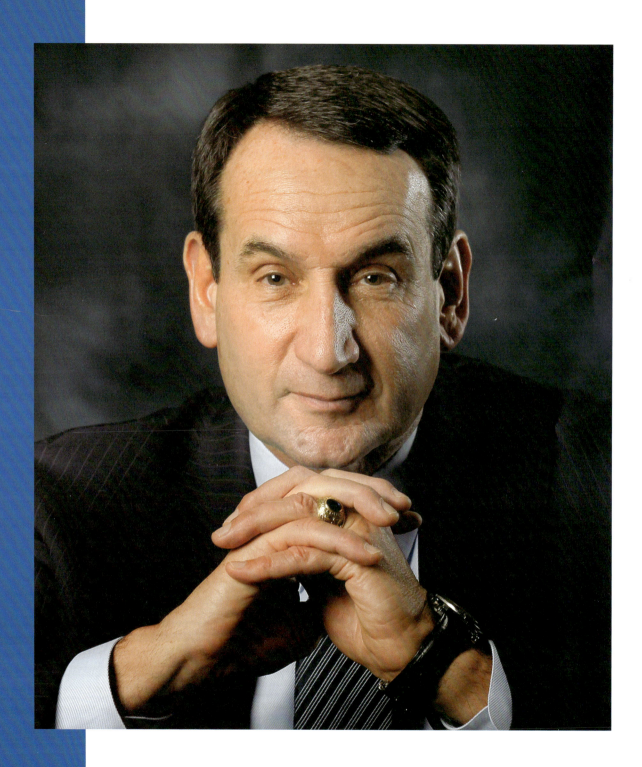

Table of Contents

OPPOSITE: At the start of the 2011-12 season, Duke coach Mike Krzyzewski had totaled 900 career victories, making him the most winning active coach in NCAA Division I history at the time. CHUCK LIDDY / THE NEWS & OBSERVER

One thousand wins and one initial: Coach K's legacy of success

BY LUKE DECOCK, THE NEWS & OBSERVER

It's easy to look back now, five NCAA titles later, and think of Mike Krzyzewski's 42 years at Duke as a constant and unrelenting ascent to the top of the college basketball world and the record books, somehow both America's Team and the Team America Loved to Hate simultaneously.

It was anything but. From a rocky start and his cold war with Dean Smith to his breakdown in 1995 to a mid-decade swoon in the 2000s, there was a surprising amount of adversity along the way, almost forgotten now in the flood of tributes (from relieved opponents) and emotion (from friends and fans and former players alike) accompanying his final departure.

But that only underlines how much Krzyzewski accomplished in four decades, from unpronounceable name to household name, from Sha-shef-ski to Coach K to simply, K. Or 1K, when he became the first major-conference men's coach to crack the 1,000-win mark.

Along the way, he went from leading a nascent rebellion against Dean Smith within the ACC to becoming everything he had rebelled against: The alpha dog of not only the ACC but college basketball in general, with the bully pulpit to match. As much as the wins, as the championships, as the legacy he leaves behind at Duke and in Durham, his longevity stands out. He surpassed his mentor, Bobby Knight. He surpassed Smith. He outlasted everyone but Jim Boeheim, who taught Krzyzewski the 2-3 zone and was his Olympic consigliere.

"To coach at one place that long," said Notre Dame coach Mike Brey, a former Krzyzewski assistant at Duke, "it'll never be heard from again."

It started 42 years ago when Steve Vacendak, a former Duke player and aide to then-athletic director Tom Butters, suggested a 33-year-old Army coach with a losing record to replace Bill Foster, who had left for South Carolina only two years after taking Duke to its first Final Four in 12 years.

Butters overruled public opinion — and

Bobby Knight's opinion; Krzyzewski's Army coach and mentor was pushing Mississippi coach Bob Weltlich, another disciple — to hire Krzyzewski, just as he did three years later when he extended Krzyzewski's contract despite an alumni uprising.

The rest — more than 1,100 wins, 15 ACC championships, 12 Final Fours, five national titles, three Olympic gold medals, one of the most influential and polarizing figures in American sports — is history, a legacy of accomplishment unmatched in the modern era of college athletics.

With Krzyzewski's ferocious sneer on the bench and punchable stars like Christian Laettner and Bobby Hurley, not to mention the smug elitism of one of America's most exclusive institutions of higher education conquering a playground game, Duke's rise to prominence made it the most loved and most hated college sports team in the country.

Krzyzewski came closest to leaving in 2004 when the Los Angeles Lakers came calling, with then-Duke president Richard

---

OPPOSITE: The Duke bench erupts in celebration as Duke clinches a victory over UNC in Cameron Indoor Stadium on March 3, 1986. JONATHAN WIGGS / THE NEWS & OBSERVER

Brodhead begging him to stay, but he would scratch the itch to coach NBA players with Team USA instead.

"Just as Mike has been good for Duke, Duke has been very good for Mike," Vacendak said. "It's been a nice marriage. People need to understand how Mike was able to expand on Duke's strengths in areas beyond basketball: Academics, alumni relations, all of that."

It was not just Duke. His family put down roots in Durham. Krzyzewski left behind not only a championship basketball program for Jon Scheyer, but the Emily K Center, which provides tutoring and mentorship for more than 2,000 Durham public-school students in the shadow of Immaculate Conception Church, where Krzyzewski has attended Sunday morning mass for four decades. His commitment was a nod not only to Durham but his upbringing on the North Side of Chicago, the son of Polish immigrants who attended a Catholic high school that no longer exists.

His legacy extends beyond basketball — the title of his SiriusXM show is "Basketball and Beyond with Coach K" — as he reached the status of the generals he went to West Point with and the CEOs who flew in for Duke's games in their private jets, not to mention the very small club of coaches that includes John Wooden and Adolph Rupp and Smith.

"I don't know if the legacy is over," Krzyzewski said. "The legacy of coaching is over."

He exits the sideline at the peak of his power, a coach who saw himself as a teacher and became an icon, known by a single letter, a monogram worth more than a thousand wins.

ABOVE: Coach Mike Krzyzewski, left, and the Duke bench cheer during the team's 91-71 win over Georgia Tech on Jan. 25, 2003, at Cameron Indoor Stadium in Durham, N.C. GRANT HALVERSON / AP PHOTO

LEFT: Travis Williams, 10, gets a little instruction from Duke head coach Mike Krzyzewski in Card Gym as they film an ad spot for the American Cancer Society, Dec. 15, 1997. CHUCK LIDDY / THE NEWS & OBSERVER

Name of the game is Kre-Shef-Ski

BY JOE TIEDE, THE NEWS & OBSERVER • PUBLISHED MARCH 20, 1980

Selection of Mike Krzyzewski as Duke's head basketball coach seemingly came as a surprise to everyone except Tom Butters and Mike Krzyzewski.

"I had a gut feeling I'd get the job," Krzyzewski admitted after he was introduced to the press Tuesday night in Durham.

"I couldn't get him out of my mind," Butters commented in reviewing the search process leading to the coaching selection.

One reason the Army coach's name escaped detection was that Butters pursued him in distant locales. The Duke athletic director first decided on an approach after talking to Indiana coach Bobby Knight. He interviewed Krzyzewski in West Lafayette, Ind., while Duke's basketball team was participating in the NCAA tournament play there. Then he talked to him in Lexington, Ky., last week during another basketball trip.

Finally, the 33-year-old coach was invited to Durham, where he met Monday with the search committee. He was offered the job that night.

Knight, Butters admitted, influenced his thinking. "Bobby assured me Mike was extremely bright and extremely talented. The more I thought about it, the better I liked the idea," he said.

"Bobby made the recommendation. My decision was made on that recommendation, in part."

In his first appearance before the area press, Krzyzewski, a black-haired Chicago native, made a favorable impression. He is clean-cut, has a pleasant speaking voice and he demonstrated a quick wit.

He kidded about his name. "You should have seen it before I changed it," he quipped.

Later, he kidded that he had one requirement for his players: "Before they graduate, they have to be able to spell my name, as well as pronounce it."

He pronounces it Kre-Shef-Ski. That's a little easier to handle than the spelling.

As expected, Coach K, as Butters likes to call him, extolled the virtues of Knight, the fiery Indiana coach whom Krzyzewski played under at West Point.

"I benefitted greatly from working with him," Krzyzewski said. "I also learned things from Dave Bliss (SMU) and Don DeVoe (Virginia Tech).

"But I'm a different person than he (Knight) is. I think the principles he teaches are excellent. But I think you make a mistake trying to be somebody else."

While Krzyzewski may adhere to Knight's reaching philosophy, he came across as quite different in personality, less serious and grim. When one writer started a question by saying, "You're obviously a shot in the dark," he fired right back, "You sound like Peter Sellers."

His quips were always followed by a smile, which had the effect of lightening the atmosphere.

Coaching in the Atlantic Coast Conference, though, tends to get serious at times.

Krzyzewski said he espoused the motion offense and man-to-man defense. He admired Duke's basketball tradition and added

---

OPPOSITE: Duke basketball coach Mike Krzyzewski looks on during a 1980 practice. JACKSON HILL / THE NEWS & OBSERVER

he'd like "to see Duke a tournament team every year."

He could draw a little comfort from the fact he was bringing with him assistant coach Bobby Dwyer, who played at Wake Forest, in the early '70s.

Butters left no doubt that the selection was his, with consent of the committee. "I feel very good about it," he said.

He also praised other candidates he had interviewed, including Bobby Wenzel, an assistant under Bill Foster. "Wenzel was definitely a viable candidate," he said. "He's a remarkable young man."

But there was something about Krzyzewski.

"I realize somebody else might have picked someone different," Butters explained. "But the chemistry seemed right to me. I want someone to fit in all areas and I think Mike will. I think players will identify very well with him."

Butters called the young coach "the brightest coaching talent in America."

Except for one year as a graduate assistant at Indiana, Krzyzewski's basketball background has been confined to West Point and military installations. He played at Army from 1967–69, then played and coached for several service teams the next five years. After the 1973–74 season at Indiana, he took the head job at Army, which had gone 3-22 the year before. His first team was 11-14, then came records of 20-8, 19-9, 14-11 and 9-17.

Recruiting, he felt, would offer more advantages than he'd been used to at Army. The possibilities at Duke obviously will be greater, but so will the expectations.

[I'd like] to see Duke a tournament team every year.

— MIKE KRZYZEWSKI

RIGHT: Mike Krzyzewski speaks to reporters as Duke athletic director Tom Butters, left, looks on at a press conference where the young coach from Army was introduced as the new basketball coach of the Blue Devils.

JACKSON HILL / THE NEWS & OBSERVER

ABOVE: Duke coach Mike Krzyzewski gives instructions to point guard Tommy Amaker during the Blue Devils game against Maryland in the 1985 ACC tournament in Atlanta, Ga. BOB BRIDGES / THE NEWS & OBSERVER

LEFT: Mike Krzyzewski waits to speak at a press conference announcing his hiring, March 18, 1980.
NEWS & OBSERVER FILE PHOTO

A general hypothetical: What if Coach K had stayed in the Army?

BY LUKE DECOCK, THE NEWS & OBSERVER • PUBLISHED NOV. 12, 2021

In 2006, Mike Krzyzewski went back to South Korea in one of his first trips with USA Basketball, taking the national team to the Army's Camp Casey ahead of the world championship in Japan. It was a return not only to the demilitarized zone, but to the path not taken.

He'd been there for the first time in 1970 as a recent graduate of the U.S. Military Academy, just out of artillery school. When he returned, he was an accomplished basketball coach climbing the record books, with three national titles to his credit and another two yet to come, not to mention three Olympic gold medals.

It was an interesting hypothetical to consider during Krzyzewski's final season at Duke when Army visited Cameron on Nov. 12, a sort of personal farewell to arms: What if he'd chosen a different uniform?

"That would never have happened," Krzyzewski says now. "I always knew I wanted to be a coach. I loved the Army. More so, if I didn't coach, I would have been

a teacher. I had my sense of duty and all that. But I didn't have a passion."

He even spent his last few years in the Army coaching — first in Korea, and then at the West Point prep school before leaving the service as a captain and joining his old Army coach, Bob Knight, as a graduate assistant at Indiana in 1974. His alma mater hired him as head coach after that 31-1 season, and the rest is history.

But what if it wasn't?

Of the 148 West Point alumni honored with the Distinguished Graduate Award, Krzyzewski is one of 36 recognized for contributions outside the military. Ninety-nine recipients retired as generals. Very broadly speaking, that's his peer group.

"He probably would have become a general," said Pat Harris, who played for Krzyzewski at Army and later followed in his footsteps as basketball coach at West Point. "There's no stopping him. He's the type of individual that adjusts well to soldiers, to players, to personnel and I think that his

flexibility truly would have helped him to be successful in the Army, too."

Harris knows of what he speaks. Not only do his personal ties to West Point run deep, two of his children served in the military as well. His son, an infantry officer, is still in the Army, stationed at Fort Bragg. Like Krzyzewski, Harris served as a field artillery officer immediately after leaving West Point. It was something they discussed as coach and player.

"He had mentioned several times that if he hadn't gotten into basketball he could have stayed in the Army," Harris said. "He enjoyed the whole thing about leading people. That's what he does in the sport of basketball. He would have had an excellent opportunity to do the same thing in the Army."

Others close to him aren't so sure. Over the course of his Duke career, Krzyzewski has frequently chafed under the strictures of the NCAA bureaucracy and railed against it, especially when it comes to what coaches can and can't do. He has shown increasing

---

OPPOSITE: Duke head basketball coach Mike Krzyzewski draws a crowd as he signs autographs for members of the U.S. Army at Funk Gym on base at Fort Bragg in Fayetteville, N.C., on Oct. 15, 2011. The Blue Devils had just finished entertaining the soldiers with a 90-minute practice session. CHUCK LIDDY / THE NEWS & OBSERVER

RIGHT: Mike Krzyzewski, left, and coach Bob Knight at West Point.
ARMY ATHLETICS

exasperation in recent years at the NCAA's failure to adapt to the quickly changing basketball world, and called for action in areas like name, image and likeness long before the NCAA was forced into change.

When it comes to bureaucracy and standing orders, the NCAA is truly following the so-called amateur model compared to the military. His daughter Jamie Spatola told The N&O's Steve Wiseman that she wasn't so sure her father would have handled that well.

"I don't know that there are any leaders that my dad admires more than military leaders," Spatola said. "He has a profound respect for service. But I don't know. I don't know if there's too many rules. I don't know. He might have been frustrated by the bureaucracy. He can feel frustrated about that at times."

There is no question, though, that some of the military lineage has run through Duke's program over these four decades. There is perhaps no better example than his relationship with Martin Dempsey, the former Chairman of the Joint Chiefs of Staff — now in his second term as chairman of USA Basketball and a Rubenstein Fellow at Duke — but it manifests in smaller ways as well.

Duke forward Joey Baker, the son of a Fort Bragg special forces sergeant, can recognize that influence implicitly.

"The things he's brought along with him from West Point are kind of instilled into the program and the culture here at Duke," Baker said. "The things that he tells us as players on a daily basis are very consistent with those values, I'd say."

Entering his fourth season at Duke in 2021–22, Baker could envision what might have happened if Krzyzewski had heeded a different call.

"I think with his attention to detail, his commitment to excellence, just his overall character, it would have lent himself to being an elite soldier, someone that serves our country in the best possible way," Baker said. "I obviously could see him being a high-ranking general, something of that sort, in the long run."

ABOVE: Duke head basketball coach Mike Krzyzewski reacts along with members of the U.S. Army at Funk Gym on base at Fort Bragg in Fayetteville, N.C., on Oct. 15, 2011. The Blue Devils were practicing in front of the troops when a "volunteer" from the crowd made a three pointer. CHUCK LIDDY / THE NEWS & OBSERVER

LEFT: Mike Krzyzewski as the head basketball coach at West Point. U.S. MILITARY ACADEMY

The day they thought Duke might fire Coach K

BY ANDREW CARTER, THE NEWS & OBSERVER • PUBLISHED MARCH 9, 2022

If Chuck Swenson goes back in time far enough he can still hear the jeers and the insults, the slurs he said some shouted from the stands during one of the longest nights of Mike Krzyzewski's coaching career, and perhaps the longest of them all. It has been almost 40 years now and Swenson has still not forgotten the things he heard that night at The Omni in Atlanta.

Usually, Swenson, who was Krzyzewski's first assistant coach at Duke, blocked it all out. That night was different. He can still hear angry Duke supporters shouting at Krzyzewski — "You're out of here; you don't know what you're doing."

That night, he thought Mike Krzyzewski might be fired.

"People were calling him 'dumb Polack,'" Swenson said during a recent phone interview. "About any name that you can think of, happened. ... Any insult or slur. There were quite a few."

It was March 11, 1983. A Friday night. The quarterfinals of the ACC tournament. Duke arrived in Atlanta a worn, beaten team in its third season under Krzyzewski. The Blue Devils had finished 3-11 in conference play, good enough for seventh place in what was then an eight-team league. Duke's prize for laboring to the end of a miserable regular season: Opening the ACC tournament against Virginia and Ralph Sampson, the Cavaliers' domineering All-American center.

It was close for a while. More than close, even. Duke held a five-point lead at one point in the first half and trailed by a manageable nine points at halftime. And then, as Swenson described it more than once recently, "the wheels came off." He could still see it in his mind all these years later, a competitive game turning into a debacle.

It ended with the most one-sided final score in ACC tournament history: Virginia 109, Duke 66.

Thirty-nine years later, it's still the most one-sided game in ACC tournament history. It was the worst loss of Krzyzewski's young career then. It's the worst loss of his Hall of Fame career now.

"The second half was ridiculous," he said afterward, according to an account the next day in the Durham Morning Herald, and in the moment he could not be sure if he'd coached his final game at Duke. At the end of his third season there, Krzyzewski was 21-34. His teams had won seven ACC games in two years. Duke reached the NCAA tournament in three consecutive seasons before his arrival, and advanced to the national championship game in 1978 and a regional final in '80.

Three years later, the Blue Devils had reached a crossroads with a young coach. It was a time long before Internet message boards and social media — places where, had they existed, Duke supporters undoubtedly would have gathered to spread vitriol, and where fans of rival schools would have joined the pile-on. Imagine the memes. The GIFs. Duke fans saying Coach K should be gone; UNC and N.C. State fans saying, no — please keep him. Disgruntled Duke fans, some of them members of the Iron Dukes,

---

OPPOSITE: Duke basketball coach Mike Krzyzewski looks on as his Blue Devils fall to Ralph Sampson and Virginia 109-66 in the 1983 ACC tournament in Greensboro, N.C.
NEWS & OBSERVER FILE PHOTO

the school's athletic booster club, voiced their displeasure in other ways.

They heckled Krzyzewski throughout that dreadful night in The Omni. They shunned him when Duke made its way back to the team hotel after the game. They attempted to convince Tom Butters, the Duke athletic director and the man who'd hired Krzyzewski, that he'd made a bad decision with that hire; that Butters should correct it sooner than later. They tried to pressure Duke to make a change, lest it fall further behind North Carolina, which won the 1982 national championship, and N.C. State, which went on to win the '83 national championship.

Swenson believed in the future. Four of Duke's top five players that season were freshmen: Johnny Dawkins, Mark Alarie, Jay Bilas and Dave Henderson. If Krzyzewski and the Blue Devils could just make it to next season, "We're going to be a lot better, I knew that," Swenson said. "The pressure was building, though, along with the impatience."

"It takes a magnifying glass to find progress," one local columnist wrote in the Durham Sun the morning after that defeat against Virginia, adding that for Duke it was "shattering, depressing and nightmarish." And that was nothing compared to what Swenson heard while he sat on the bench in The Omni, the minutes winding down in an ugly defeat, and perhaps in his time at Duke.

Sitting there, Swenson recalls, "I said, 'Crap.' That's the first time I thought we might not make it to next year. And that's the first time it really hit me."

Duke AD was patient with Krzyzewski

There's an alternate universe out there where Krzyzewski doesn't last at Duke beyond 1983. One where some big-money Iron Duke, or maybe a few of them, come up with a lot of money to turn their displeasure into action. One where Butters, the athletic director, has no choice but to relent to the pressure. It didn't happen that way but the question is worth considering nonetheless:

What if Coach K didn't make it to a fourth season?

It seems like a preposterous question now and in a way it was then, too, given Butters' unwavering support. Krzyzewski has talked about that a lot recently, how Butters stood by him when few others did. It came up again last week, in the days before Krzyzewski's final game at Cameron Indoor Stadium, and undoubtedly it will resurface throughout his last March — the story of how Krzyzewski wondered if he'd make it to 1984 at Duke, let alone 39 more years there.

During a long interview in his office before the season began, Krzyzewski went back to that night in The Omni. Along with missing most of the 1994–95 season due to back surgery and mental exhaustion, he considered that loss against Virginia to be "one of the two lowest points of my 42 years" at Duke.

"Walking off the court in Atlanta," he said, "with a lot of the Iron Dukes wanting me fired. And again, I never felt I would be. Because of my relationship (with Butters). But, one, we had these good young players, but then obviously you're very naive, too.

"I always believed we were going to win. But we hadn't."

He was sitting in a six-story tower built in 1999, one whose very existence was a testament to all the winning he'd done over the past 39 years. In that setting, then, it was easier to imagine a world at Duke without Krzyzewski, one in which he'd been told to leave in 1983. Imagine the photos along the walls of his office, those capturing celebratory moments after championships, fading away like a special effect in Back to the Future. Imagine a Duke campus without this office tower at all.

No Coach K Court at Cameron. No Krzyzewskiville, or perhaps it exists somewhere else.

When he looked out onto Krzyzewskiville on Saturday, before his final home game, Krzyzewski took a moment to store the memory away in his mind. The rectangular lawn was filled to capacity, a Duke blue sea of humanity that danced and drank and gathered to see him work one last time. Hours later, when Krzyzewski appeared on the court before his final game, it was almost like a religious experience for the people who'd come to send him off. All that for a man some were so sure should be fired after that 43-point loss against Virginia in 1983.

"And how do you think they feel now?" Bilas said of those doubters.

These days Jay Bilas is an ESPN college basketball analyst, one of the leading voices of the sport. Back then, after his freshman year, he wondered if the coach who convinced him to come to Duke might be gone. Bilas had moved across the country to Durham, from outside of Los Angeles, because he believed in the vision that Krzyzewski had sold him on the future.

Now that future was in doubt.

"There's more than a couple times where I called home and said, 'What do I do if they fire him?'" Bilas said recently. "'I'm not staying here if they fire the coach. I'm leaving.' And my dad had to tell me, 'Just play. There's nothing you can do about it — just play.'

"But I do remember the following year, when he signed an extension. He came in the locker room and said, 'I just signed an extension, so everything's good.' And we just went out practiced and that was the end of it. But it took until then."

The extension arrived in late January of 1984. The Blue Devils, who'd spent the previous two seasons near the bottom of the ACC standings, were starting to show signs of improvement, though they'd just endured a 31-point loss at Wake Forest. Still, Duke was 14-4 when the school announced Krzyzewski's new deal, a five-year contract through the 1988–89 season.

"He deserved it, he's earned it," Butters said then, according to the Durham Morning Herald.

The extension ended speculation about Krzyzewski's short-term future. Soon enough, there'd be no doubts at all. Still, Bilas said, for a while "there was an air around here. And the truth is, we didn't care too much for our fan base at that time. Because they weren't supportive of him."

How Krzyzewski defines himself

Krzyzewski's coaching legacy has been defined by victories and memorable triumphs, the years and years of sustained success. The five national championships. The 12 Final Fours. The 15 ACC tournament titles. He has won nearly 1,200 games, and become as synonymous with Duke as any figure ever has with any particular institution.

Krzyzewski the man, though, has been most defined by more difficult times.

"Reference points," he called them. Those moments in which people can go in one direction or another. When the future is less certain than it is in the good times. In the early 1980s, there weren't a lot of good times for Krzyzewski at Duke. The victory against North Carolina at home during his first season was the high point, and then came 34 defeats over the next two seasons.

"To me, reference points are not as much victories as they are setbacks," Krzyzewski said.

Back then, in the years after he arrived at Duke in 1980, Krzyzewski spent a lot of time, in his words, "learning about the neighborhood." It was his way of describing the dynamic then among UNC, Duke and N.C. State, three schools within about 30 miles of one another.

At UNC, Dean Smith had already become one of the country's great coaches, and he won the first of his two national championships in 1982. At N.C. State, Jim Valvano arrived the same year that Krzyzewski did at Duke. The Wolfpack's national championship in 1983, as improbable as it was, was its second in school history. The Blue Devils had yet to win one.

The UNC-N.C. State basketball rivalry, and not the one between UNC and Duke, was the fiercest in the state. It was a different time — and though success has long become the norm at Duke, it wasn't so much back then, especially after the Blue Devils

faltered in Krzyzewski's earliest seasons. Part of those struggles were attributable to a young coach learning how to figure it out. Part of them could be explained by the competition.

"The ACC was unbelievable," Krzyzewski said. "It's not like there were bad teams — there were great teams."

The league's collection of coaches in those days was arguably as strong as it has ever been, too. Smith at UNC. Valvano at N.C. State. Terry Holland at Virginia. Lefty Driesell at Maryland.

And then, at Duke, the young guy from Army with the difficult-to-pronounce name.

"I think I've always been trying to prove myself," Krzyzewski said. "And so I really needed to at that time."

Krzyzewski never forgot

Back in The Omni that night in 1983, Virginia proved relentless in the second half. The Cavaliers played as if they were angry. Perhaps they were. Afterward, Sampson accused the Blue Devils, and Bilas in particular, of playing dirty in the first half, an assertion Bilas denied. There was no arguing the scoreboard, though.

After halftime, Virginia outscored Duke 59-25.

John Feinstein, then a young reporter with The Washington Post, began his game story like this:

"It does not pay to tug on Superman's

cape. Or on Ralph Sampson's jersey."

As its margin increased, from a 20-point lead, to 30 and beyond, Virginia showed no mercy.

"I felt they rubbed our noses in it, to be quite honest," Swenson said, and then came all the angst from Duke supporters. It wasn't so much the university's administration that Swenson feared but "the alumni, the money givers that scared me."

He could remember that Krzyzewski was "solemn" afterward, that he was "compassionate" toward his players, who'd just been humiliated. In the moment, Swenson said, Krzyzewski was "ready to move on," and yet it was a defeat, too, that lingered in a variety of ways.

Krzyzewski has coached almost 1,600 games. Few take him back more vividly to a certain moment in time than that one on March 11, 1983, so that he can feel what he felt then, and relive it in a way that allows him to contextualize how that loss helped fuel him, and the rise of his program.

"Our guys never forgot that," said Swenson, who remained an assistant at Duke through 1987. "And K's really good about reminding people about what happens, and when they didn't play hard enough or they were embarrassed, or whatever positive or negative, he's good at remembering.

"And I can't remember the number, but it took a long time for Virginia to beat us

> ## I think I've always been trying to prove myself. And so I really needed to at that time.
>
> — MIKE KRZYZEWSKI

after that."

It didn't happen again for the rest of the 1980s. Krzyzewski lost his first seven games against Virginia, a run of futility that ended with the worst defeat of his career. Then he led Duke to 16 consecutive victories against the Cavaliers, who didn't beat Duke again until February 1990.

By then Duke was on its way. The Blue Devils' first national championship came a little more than a year later. Then their second, the year after that. Krzyzewski became one of the most successful and recognizable figures in his sport, and gradually became one of the leading faces of it, the defining personality of an internationally known university.

Krzyzewski's influence is all over Duke's campus in Durham. The things that are named after him. The buildings that might not exist if not for what he became. And all after everything appeared so tenuous after one particular game in 1983. That defeat against Virginia represented the end point of a difficult season and, in a way, of an era of sustained struggle early in Krzyzewski's career.

"That score was brought up a lot by Coach K," Bilas said. "It was on the scoreboard at the first practice the next year, on Oct. 15. It said 109-66 on the scoreboard.

"So it wasn't something we were inclined to forget."

Krzyzewski never did. Not then. Not now.

In the rubble of the worst loss of his career, he laid a foundation for what was to come.

Johnny Dawkins

Years at Duke: 1983–86
NBA Draft pick: No. 10
Team: San Antonio Spurs

Why his Duke jersey is retired

Duke didn't begin its rise to national prominence under Mike Krzyzewski until Dawkins arrived on campus. It wasn't a coincidence. He averaged at least 18.1 points per game in each of his four seasons and left school as its all-time leading scorer.

Before Dawkins arrived in Durham, some wondered whether Coach K was the right man for the job. By the time Dawkins left, having led Duke to the 1986 national title game, the Blue Devils had become a national power.

His jersey was retired Feb. 22, 1986.

Duke stats and achievements

• Averaged 19.2 points, 4.2 assists and 4 rebounds in his career
• Scored 2,556 career points
• Naismith Player of the Year (1986)
• Consensus first-team All-American (1985, 1986)

RIGHT: Johnny Dawkins passes during first-half action against St. Louis, Jan. 8, 1986. SCOTT SHARPE / THE NEWS & OBSERVER

ABOVE: Duke point guard Johnny Dawkins rides on the shoulders of a Duke fan after the Blue Devils defeated Georgia Tech 68-67 to win the ACC basketball tournament on March 9, 1986, in Greensboro, N.C. ROBERT WILLETT / THE NEWS & OBSERVER

ABOVE LEFT: Duke Coach Mike Krzyzewski, left, hugs tournament MVP Johnny Dawkins after Duke defeated Georgia Tech to win the ACC tournament on March 9, 1986. It was Krzyzewski's first ACC tournament championship. NEWS & OBSERVER FILE PHOTO

LEFT: From left, Duke coaches Johnny Dawkins, Mike Krzyzewski and Steve Wojciechowski call to the Blue Devils as the Devils battle out an 83-81 overtime win over the Tar Heels, Feb. 5, 2004. SCOTT LEWIS / THE NEWS & OBSERVER

Danny Ferry

Years at Duke: 1985–89
NBA Draft pick: No. 2
Team: Los Angeles Clippers

Why his Duke jersey is retired

Like Johnny Dawkins, Ferry became one of Duke's first national stars during the first decade of Krzyzewski's tenure. Ferry played a supporting role on the Blue Devils' 1986 Final Four team, and then was among the best players in the nation over his final two seasons.

Ferry led Duke to the 1989 Final Four, when he earned National Player of the Year honors, and he remains one of two Blue Devils to be named ACC Player of the Year in back-to-back seasons.

His jersey was retired Feb. 18, 1989.

Duke stats and achievements

- Averaged 22.6 points and 7.2 rebounds as a senior
- National player of the year (1989)
- Consensus first-team All-American (1989)
- ACC Player of the Year (1988, 1989)
- Reached two Final Fours

RIGHT: Duke forward Danny Ferry flips in a layup against Maryland's Tony Massenburg in 1989 at Cameron Indoor Stadium. GARY ALLEN / THE NEWS & OBSERVER

LEFT: Duke's Danny Ferry drives to the basket against Boston University during NCAA tournament action in the Smith Center, March 17, 1988.
GENE FURR / THE NEWS & OBSERVER

Overdue Duke KOs KU to win first national championship

BY CHIP ALEXANDER, THE NEWS & OBSERVER • PUBLISHED APRIL 2, 1991

INDIANAPOLIS — At long last, Duke's time has come. The Blue Devils are the national basketball champions.

Let it ring loud because it's true: National champions.

With a 72-65 victory over Kansas in the NCAA finals Monday night at the Hoosier Dome, Duke finally has achieved a dream that has endured over four decades. After nine trips to the Final Four, after four runner-up finishes, the Blue Devils have done it.

A hastily made handmade sign may have put it best. It read: "We believe — bridesmaids no more."

No more frustration, no more talk about Final Four failure or the "monkey" on Coach Mike Krzyzewski's back. The Devils simply would not put up with it any longer, upsetting haughty Nevada-Las Vegas in the semifinals Saturday and then on Monday refusing to be satisfied with that oh-so-glorious win over the defending NCAA champs.

"I'm not sure anyone has ever played any harder for 80 minutes than we did," said Krzyzewski, who has taken Duke to four straight Final Fours and five of the last six.

"Kansas is a courageous team that was ready to play. After watching them in warm-ups, I told my staff, 'This is going to be a helluva game; I hope we have enough left.' To beat them when they were playing so hard makes the championship even better."

And that monkey?

"There has never been a monkey on my back," Krzyzewski replied. "I've always tried to keep all that in perspective.

"I'm just happy and proud of my team. I love this group, and to see their faces and the happiness was great."

Krzyzewski smiled.

"We played really good basketball in March," he said. "I'm glad to say we finally played good basketball in April."

Duke's march to the Final Four included victories over Northeast Louisiana, Iowa, Connecticut and St. John's in the Midwest Regional. Then came the emotional victory over UNLV, which smashed the Devils by 30 points in last year's championship game, followed by an impressive, wire-to-wire win in the final.

Junior Christian Laettner, Duke's big man in so many ways, had 18 points and 10 rebounds as the Blue Devils put the finishing touches on a special 32-7 season. Laettner, 12-for-12 at the line, always a man under the boards, fittingly enough was named the most outstanding player of the Final Four, easily erasing any disappointment he may have had in not being named Atlantic Coast Conference player of the year.

"All I care about is the national championship and giving that trophy to Coach to take back to Duke," Laettner said. "We won it for the team, for our fans — for Duke."

Billy McCaffrey, big off the bench, gave the Devils another 16 points. The sophomore guard, ever confident, hit six of eight shots and nearly every basket seemed critical against Kansas' overplaying defense.

"Billy was magnificent," Krzyzewski said. "He picked a great game to show his stuff

OPPOSITE: Duke coach Mike Krzyzewski holds up the national championship trophy to the crowd during a celebration in Cameron Indoor Stadium, April 2, 1991.
CHRIS SEWARD / THE NEWS & OBSERVER

again, and if he doesn't hit, I'm not sure we score very much."

And what can you say about Duke's Bobby Hurley?

Hurley, who has matured so much this season, was at his best with the championship on the line. The sophomore point guard contributed 12 points and nine assists, but his leadership, precision ball-handling, defense and poise in the NCAA tournament transcended mere statistics.

"In the last two games, Vegas and Kansas played the best man-to-man defense we've seen all year," Krzyzewski said. "For Bobby to play the way he did, with so few turnovers, was remarkable.

"He played 80 minutes in the Final Four. I can't imagine how he did it so well."

Duke led 42-34 at halftime, built the margin to 14 points with less than nine minutes to play and weathered a late Kansas threat. The Jayhawks, 27-8, trimmed the lead to 70-65 with 35 seconds left and nearly caused a 10-second backcourt violation before Duke's Thomas Hill alertly called for a time-out with 25.7 seconds left.

On the in-bounds play, Duke's Brian Davis made a quick break to the basket, Grant Hill's pass was true and Davis slammed it through with 23 seconds to play. Kansas missed two shots and a tap, and soon it was over.

Senior Mark Randall, who played for Krzyzewski on the U.S. national team last summer, finished with 18 points and 10 rebounds for the Jayhawks, who dumped North Carolina in the semifinals. Senior guard Terry Brown, he of the funky jump shot, added 16 points but was just six-of-15 from the field as Kansas shot 41.5 percent.

"Everything we tried, Duke had an answer for," said Kansas coach Roy Williams, whose team tied for the Big Eight Conference regular-season title. "But what we've done in the past three weeks, beating teams like Indiana, Arkansas and Carolina, was amazing.

"The only team in the country that would not trade places with Kansas is Duke. The only guy in America luckier than Roy Williams is Mike Krzyzewski."

And more than lucky. Talented. The consummate team.

And now champions. National champions.

Duke 72, Kansas 65

PLAYER	MP	FG	FGA	FG%	2P	2PA	2P%	3P	3PA	3P%	FT	FTA	FT%	ORB	DRB	TRB	AST	STL	BLK	TOV	PF	PTS
Bobby Hurley	40	3	5	.600	1	1	1.000	2	4	.500	4	4	1.000	0	1	1	9	2	0	3	1	12
Christian Laettner	32	3	8	.375	3	8	.375	0	0		12	12	1.000	4	6	10	0	1	0	4	3	18
Grant Hill	28	4	6	.667	4	6	.667	0	0		2	8	.250	0	8	8	3	2	2	2	1	10
Thomas Hill	23	1	5	.200	0	4	.000	1	1	1.000	0	0		0	4	4	1	0	0	0	2	3
Greg Koubek	17	2	4	.500	1	2	.500	1	2	.500	0	0		2	2	4	0	1	0	2	1	5
Bill McCaffrey	26	6	8	.750	4	5	.800	2	3	.667	2	2	1.000	0	1	1	0	0	0	4	1	16
Brian Davis	24	4	5	.800	4	5	.800	0	0		0	2	.000	0	2	2	1	0	0	1	4	8
Crawford Palmer	9	0	0		0	0		0	0		0	0		0	0	0	0	0	0	1	0	0
Antonio Lang	1	0	0		0	0		0	0		0	0		0	0	0	0	0	0	1	0	0
TOTAL	200	23	41	.561	17	31	.548	6	10	.600	20	28	.714	6	24	30	14	6	2	18	13	72

Everything we tried,
Duke had an answer for.

— KANSAS COACH ROY WILLIAMS

LEFT: Duke point guard Bobby Hurley works around pressure from UNC's King Rice in a 1991 game at Duke. CHUCK LIDDY / THE NEWS & OBSERVER

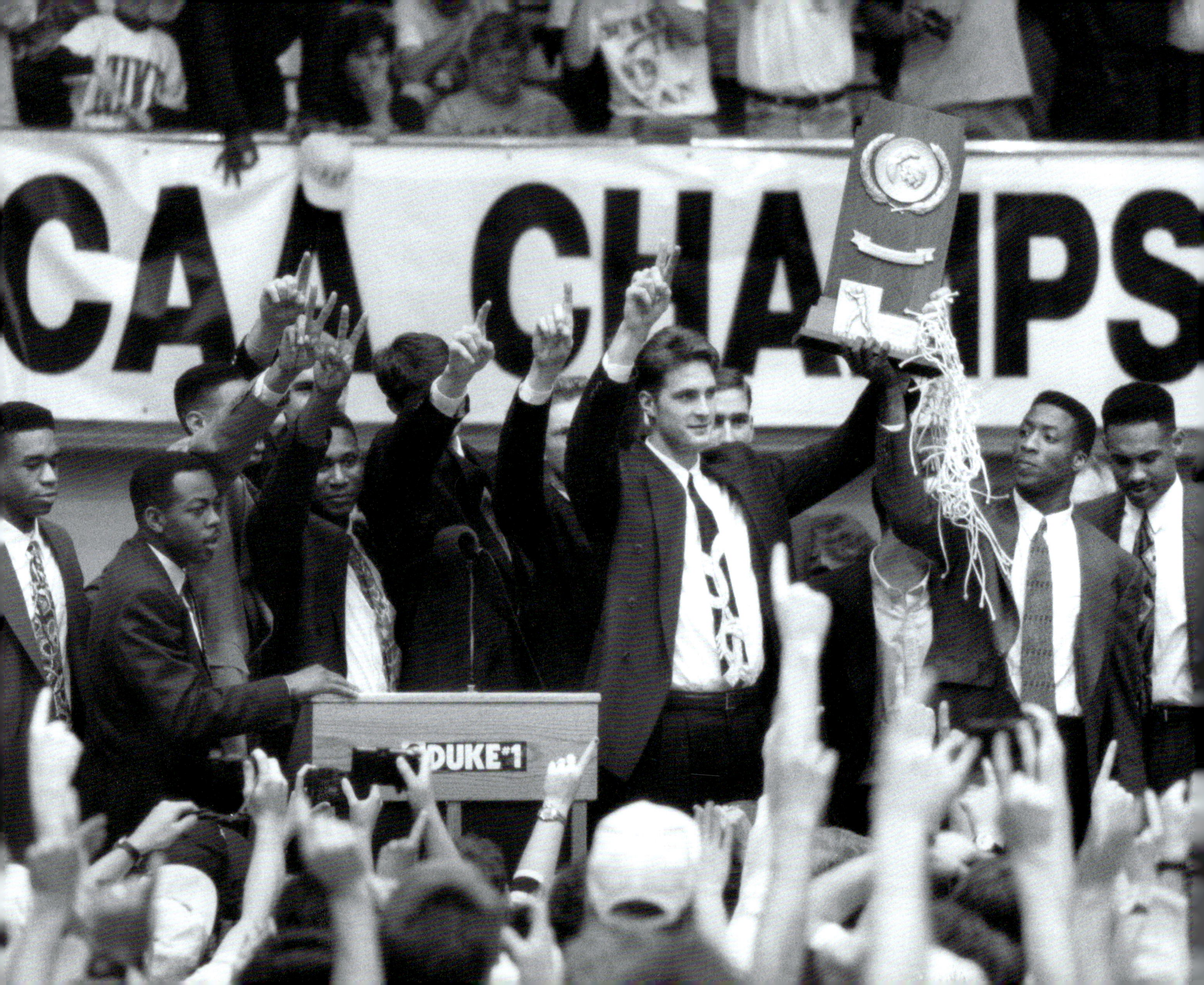
CAA CHAMPS
DUKE #1

Give Devils their two! Duke uses grit to win it

BY DANE HUFFMAN, THE NEWS & OBSERVER • PUBLISHED APRIL 7, 1992

MINNEAPOLIS — Duke, for all its glamour and all its glitz, has always been a team with grit. And Monday night in a ragged fight for the NCAA title with Michigan, the Devils used that determination to do the dirty work of winning, to win 71-51 and claim a special part of college history.

"It wasn't the prettiest game," said Duke's Bobby Hurley, "but we were resilient out there. We got the job done."

Duke became the first college basketball team to win consecutive national titles since UCLA in 1973.

"They're a most deserving champion," said Bill Walton, a center who was a cornerstone of that Bruin dynasty. "They're one of the finest college basketball teams I've seen in a long time."

Duke dominated this season, coming off its 1991 title to be ranked No. 1 all year. And against a brutal schedule, the Devils posted a 34-2 record and finished with their fingers on the championship trophy again.

Roy Kramer, the chairman of the NCAA selection committee, appeared to let the trophy slip a bit as he handed it to Duke coach Mike Krzyzewski on the podium. But Krzyzewski quickly grabbed it — glad to have the precious slab of wood after such a long pursuit — and hoisted the prize for what remained of the Metrodome crowd of 50,739 to see.

"They're the best," Krzyzewski said of his team, which overcame injuries to six of its top seven players to win the title. "And they deserve it. I'm so proud of them."

Michigan's valiant freshmen were unfazed at being center stage with the team that has dominated the college game. The confident and oh-so-talented Wolverines, 88-85 losers in overtime to Duke early in the season, charged right at the Blue Devils and the game that followed was a raw, ragged affair.

Duke had 12 turnovers in the first half alone and couldn't find an offensive rhythm. Christian Laettner, the Blue Devil senior whose brilliant game slayed Kentucky, spent the entire first half in an uncharacteristic funk.

He had scored only eight points in the semifinal win over Indiana, and many expected the 6-foot-11 center to come back with a fury against the Wolverines. But Laettner played a tentative first half. He missed his first shot, a 3-pointer, and saw his second shot, another three, clang off the side of the backboard.

He wasn't looking once and a Grant Hill pass just bounced right off him. And, when double-teamed, his passes out of the post were often picked off by Michigan defenders.

"Obviously I was frustrated," Laettner said, "not because I was missing shots, but because I was hurting our team. My turnovers were leading to their buckets."

By halftime, Laettner had only five points and Michigan had a 31-30 lead. It might have been worse if Hurley, the Most Outstanding Player of the Final Four, and Thomas Hill didn't hit key shots to keep the Devils going.

But the Blue Devils needed their star to get going if they didn't want to hear the echoes the Michigan fight song all summer.

OPPOSITE: The national champions raise the NCAA trophy and the game net into the air at their welcome home ceremony in Cameron Indoor Stadium, April 7, 1992.
SCOTT SHARPE / THE NEWS & OBSERVER

"Christian had his worst half of the year," Krzyzewski said. "His play in the second half was the difference in the game."

Laettner went right to work. Michigan (25-9) turned the ball over on its first possession and Laettner hustled downcourt to take a pass from Hurley in transition and score on a driving layup.

"Bobby made that fantastic pass," Krzyzewski said, "and Christian caught it. I thought that helped him."

It certainly seemed to get Laettner rolling, and he came back on Duke's next possession to hit a 3-pointer and give Duke the lead for good at 35-33.

Laettner seemed more fresh, more alive, in the second half, and he clamped onto Wolverine freshman Chris Webber and wouldn't let Webber get the ball. Webber tortured Duke with 27 points in that game in Ann Arbor, Mich., but Monday, he had only 14.

The Blue Devils held Michigan to nine-for-31 (29 percent) from the floor in the second half.

"I thought we played with much more emotion in the second half," Krzyzewski said. "And we didn't turn it over. We were very efficient, offensively, in the second half."

Steve Fisher, the Michigan coach who tried for his second title in four years, also thought Duke's defense was critical in the second half.

"In the second half we had no semblance of order on offense," Fisher said. "And I think it was as much their defense as anything. We unraveled with some bad shots, and you can't do that against a really good team. We had difficulties finding any way to get easy baskets, and you have to get some easy baskets if you are going to have a chance against this team."

Laettner finished with 19 points to lead the Devils in his final game in royal blue. Grant Hill, who constantly drove down the left baseline against the Michigan defense, had 18 points and also five assists.

Duke 71, Michigan 51

PLAYER	MP	FG	FGA	FG%	2P	2PA	2P%	3P	3PA	3P%	FT	FTA	FT%	ORB	DRB	TRB	AST	STL	BLK	TOV	PF	PTS
Grant Hill	37	8	14	.571	8	14	.571	0	0		2	2	1.000	5	5	10	5	3	2	3	2	18
Bobby Hurley	37	3	12	.250	2	9	.222	1	3	.333	2	2	1.000	0	3	3	7	1	0	3	4	9
Christian Laettner	36	6	13	.462	4	9	.444	2	4	.500	5	6	.833	1	6	7	0	1	1	7	1	19
Thomas Hill	35	5	10	.500	4	8	.500	1	2	.500	5	8	.625	3	4	7	0	2	0	0	2	16
Antonio Lang	32	2	3	.667	2	3	.667	0	0		1	2	.500	2	2	4	0	1	0	0	1	5
Cherokee Parks	13	1	3	.333	1	3	.333	0	0		2	2	1.000	2	1	3	0	0	1	1	3	4
Brian Davis	10	0	2	.000	0	2	.000	0	0		0	0		0	0	0	0	1	0	0	0	0
Christian Ast	0	0	0		0	0		0	0		0	0		0	1	1	0	0	0	0	0	0
Kenny Blakeney	0	0	0		0	0		0	0		0	0		0	0	0	0	0	0	0	0	0
Ron Burt	0	0	0		0	0		0	0		0	0		0	0	0	0	0	0	0	0	0
Marty Clark	0	0	0		0	0		0	0		0	0		0	0	0	0	0	0	0	0	0
TOTAL	200	25	57	.439	21	48	.438	4	9	.444	17	22	.773	13	22	35	12	9	4	14	13	71

They're a most deserving champion. They're one of the finest college basketball teams I've seen in a long time.

— BILL WALTON

LEFT: Duke's Grant Hill dunks against Florida State's Chuck Graham. SCOTT SHARPE / THE NEWS & OBSERVER

Duke center Christian Laettner (32) fires up a shot over Kentucky's Deron Feldhaus with .2 seconds left on the game clock to score and sending the Blue Devils to the Final Four on March 28, 1992, beating the Wildcats in overtime 104-103. Grant Hill threw a pass the length of the court to Laettner, who faked right, dribbled once, turned and hit a jumper as time expired for the 104-103 win.

CHUCK LIDDY / THE NEWS & OBSERVER

LEFT: Duke coach Mike Krzyzewski and the Blue Devils hoist the national championship trophy. CHUCK LIDDY / THE NEWS & OBSERVER

Christian Laettner

Years at Duke: 1988–92
NBA Draft pick: No. 3
Team: Minnesota Timberwolves

Why his Duke jersey is retired

Few players in the history of college basketball have exceeded or matched what Laettner did at Duke. He was a part of four Final Four teams, and in time became the national face of the sport. He led the Blue Devils to consecutive national championships during his final two seasons.

He made arguably the most iconic shot in NCAA tournament history, the turnaround at the buzzer in overtime to beat Kentucky and send Duke to the 1992 Final Four. Think of the definitive player of the Coach K era, and Laettner is probably the first to come to mind.

His jersey was retired Feb. 26, 1992.

Duke stats and achievements

- 21.5 ppg as a senior
- 2,460 career points
- National champion (1991, 1992)
- Consensus National Player of the Year (1992)
- Final Four Most Outstanding Player (1991)

RIGHT: Duke's Brian Davis, left, embraces teammate Christian Laettner as the Blue Devils defeat Georgia Tech in the 1992 ACC tournament.
NEWS & OBSERVER FILE PHOTO

ABOVE: Former Duke player Danny Ferry guards Christian Laettner during a charity game held at Cameron Indoor Stadium, Aug. 23, 2002. CHUCK LIDDY / THE NEWS & OBSERVER

LEFT: Duke forward Christian Laettner attempts a layup against Clemson. NEWS & OBSERVER FILE PHOTO

Bobby Hurley

Years at Duke: 1989–93
NBA Draft pick: No. 7
Team: Sacramento Kings

Why his Duke jersey is retired

It's impossible to think of Christian Laettner or Grant Hill or those championship Duke teams of the early 1990s without also thinking of Hurley, who made everything go. From the start, he was Krzyzewski's first great point guard at Duke.

He led the Blue Devils from his first college game, starting all 38 games as a freshman, and helped lead Duke to the 1990 Final Four before the back-to-back titles the next two years. Almost 30 years after his final college game, Hurley is still college basketball's all-time leader in assists.

His jersey was retired Feb. 28, 1993.

Duke stats and achievements

- Averaged 17 points and 8.2 assists as a senior
- Holds NCAA career assists record with 1,076
- Final Four Most Outstanding Player (1992)
- National champion (1991, 1992)
- Consensus first-team All-American (1993)

RIGHT: Bobby Hurley salutes the crowd at his final game in 1993.
NEWS & OBSERVER FILE PHOTO

ABOVE: Duke point guard Bobby Hurley attempts to elude Cal's Akili Jones in a 1993 game.
CHUCK LIDDY / THE NEWS & OBSERVER

LEFT: Duke's Bobby Hurley waves to the crowd during his final game in Cameron Indoor Stadium, March 4, 1993. ROBERT WILLETT / THE NEWS & OBSERVER

Grant Hill

Years at Duke: 1990–94
NBA Draft pick: No. 3
Team: Detroit Pistons

Why his Duke jersey is retired

Remember the three-quarter-court pass to Christian Laettner with 2.1 seconds left that set up the game-winning shot against Kentucky in the 1992 Elite Eight? That was Grant Hill's arm that delivered it.

Hill earned freshman All-American and freshman All-ACC honors on Duke's first national championship team in 1991 and made three Final Four appearances, leading the Blue Devils back there in 1994 as a senior.

His jersey was retired Feb. 27, 1994.

Duke stats and achievements

- Averaged 17.4 points, 6.9 rebounds and 5.2 assists as a senior
- His 591 points led the ACC in scoring in 1993–94
- National champion (1991, 1992)
- Consensus first-team All-American (1994)
- Consensus second-team All-American (1993)

RIGHT: Duke's Grant Hill brings the ball up the court under pressure from Maryland's Vince Broadnax in a 1992 game. SCOTT SHARPE / THE NEWS & OBSERVER

ABOVE: Duke freshman Grant Hill drives to the basket during a 1990 game against Marquette at Cameron Indoor Stadium. CHRIS SEWARD / THE NEWS & OBSERVER

LEFT: Duke's Grant Hill flies toward the basket for a dunk in 1991. ROBERT WILLETT / THE NEWS & OBSERVER

1995: A season that turned two coaches' fates

BY LUKE DECOCK, THE NEWS & OBSERVER • PUBLISHED MAY 22, 2005

A decade ago this week, Pete Gaudet walked away from Duke basketball after a dozen years as Mike Krzyzcwski's top assistant and closed the door on one of the strangest seasons in the program's history.

His name forever will be entwined with what happened at Duke in 1995, when the Blue Devils went 13-18 and Gaudet spent three months as interim coach after Krzyzewski was hospitalized for exhaustion.

"I don't think about it. I don't talk about it," said Gaudet, 63, who now is a member of the women's basketball staff at Ohio State.

"It's just kind of part of my past."

For Krzyzewski, the lessons learned amid the wreckage of 1995 still resonate. He has spent the past decade retooling both the Duke program and his approach to life with tangible results. An unheralded Duke team won the 2005 ACC tournament title; next year, the Devils hope to win a national title.

It is no coincidence two of his assistant coaches — Steve Wojciechowski and Chris Collins — played on the 1995 team.

They know, as Krzyzewski does now, that Duke's tradition is fragile and success is not guaranteed.

"It seems like that never happened. I know it did, but it's gone by fast, let's put it that way," Krzyzewski said. "I still have a hard time understanding I'm 58, because it goes by fast. If you love what you do and you throw yourself into that, all of a sudden it's another season, that type of thing.

"But certainly what happened 10 years ago helps shape for me a better understanding and a better perspective of what you have to do to maintain something at a real high level."

What happened 10 years ago threatened all that Krzyzewski had built in his first 15 years at Duke. Overburdened and overcommitted, he was hospitalized for exhaustion after 12 games, and the Devils finished last in the ACC under Gaudet. Watching the disaster, Krzyzewski learned the Duke brand he created, without a change in philosophy, would wither without him.

When Krzyzewski went to his first Final Four in 1986, he was a young, insightful coach who had restored the pride of a traditional power. By 1992, when the Devils won their second straight NCAA title, he had become a national figure, with national demands on his time. He had charitable causes to support, personal appearances to make and books to write.

That summer, he served as an assistant coach on the Dream Team in Barcelona, winning an Olympic gold medal but working through an entire offseason. Krzyzewski was gambling his stamina could hold out, that his body and mind could hold up.

In 1995, he lost.

A wife's ultimatum

In October 1994, Krzyzewski had surgery to correct a bulging disk in his lower back. He hurried back, against the advice of his doctors, but his players weren't fooled. Collins, then a Duke junior, saw a different look in his coach's eyes that fall — fatigue.

He wasn't the only one to see it. On Jan. 5,

OPPOSITE: Duke University head basketball coach Mike Krzyzewski announces that his longtime assistant coach Pete Gaudet will be stepping down during a press conference in the Duke locker room, May 19, 1995. ROBERT WILLETT / THE NEWS & OBSERVER

ESTABLISHING A DYNASTY • 41

1995, Krzyzewski's wife Mickie delivered him an ultimatum: her or basketball. As she would later explain, her 47-year-old husband looked "80 years old, gray-looking, hunched over."

The next day, he was hospitalized. Duke was 9-3 when the program was turned over to Gaudet.

Three games into his tenure, Duke blew a 23-point second-half lead to Virginia at home, one of nine straight losses to open the ACC slate. By the time it was over, Duke set a school record for losses.

"Miserable," Collins called it.

For other Duke teams, Krzyzewski's absence may not have been insurmountable. Earlier in the 1990s, his teams had leaders such as Bobby Hurley, Brian Davis, Christian Laettner and Grant Hill. After Hill graduated in 1994, the only seniors were forward Cherokee Parks, an offbeat Californian, and role players Kenny Blakeney and Erik Meek.

"Those guys, for whatever reason, didn't do a good job," said Virginia Commonwealth coach Jeff Capel III, a sophomore in 1995. (Parks, through his agent, could not be reached for comment.)

Still, the upperclassmen on the 1995 team all had been to at least one Final Four. The freshmen included Trajan Langdon and Wojciechowski. And Gaudet, a former Army head coach, tutored big men such as Laettner and Danny Ferry and had in the past been able to keep the team loose with a keen wit.

It wasn't enough to overcome the sense of entitlement that had enveloped the Duke program. Collins admits the 1995 team took winning for granted.

"You learn you make those things happen," he said. "The players and the coaches make that happen. It's not just a rite of passage. I think that's a lesson that the players in 1995 had to learn, and we didn't have our leader there to snap us out of it. When everything hit the fan, we didn't have the rock or the foundation that was always there, who knew the right buttons to push. We didn't have the right instincts of what our team needed."

Gaudet resigned after the season to teach in Duke's physical education department. Another assistant, Mike Brey, left to become the head coach at Delaware and is now at Notre Dame.

With a wife and three children, Gaudet had been the team's "restricted earnings coach" despite being the senior assistant and made just $16,000 a year. A week after he resigned, the NCAA — prodded by a federal judge's response to lawsuits filed by Gaudet and other coaches — ended the salary restrictions.

Gaudet did not pursue a return to his old job.

"At that point, you make a decision, and all of a sudden, it's settled," he said. "It's hard to say everything is OK as it was. I had taken a new step, and just like a lot of other things in life where you make a decision — an old girlfriend calls, or something like that — I made the decision and this was the direction we were going in, that all parties were going in. It was kind of a moot point."

K's life redefined

As Gaudet had been coaching the team, Krzyzewski had been reprioritizing his life on and off court. He redirected his energy from building a winning team to building a winning program and preventing another collapse.

"We didn't want to be back to where we were before. We wanted to be better," he said. "We wanted to be more well-rounded. We wanted to have a broader base than what our program was doing. It wasn't just about trying to win an ACC championship or whatever. It was trying to be more a part of the university community and the community at large.

"It was a better plan, and part of it is probably because I had time to think. Going to seven Final Fours in nine years, you don't have time to think about anything else. ... Probably someone else would have, but I couldn't. Being out like that gave me an opportunity to look at it with a broader stroke."

Krzyzewski gave up management of ancillary areas of his job, from community involvement to charitable causes, to concentrate on his family and his basketball team. Once praised for his accessibility, he continued to withdraw from the local media.

Instead of hiring assistants from other programs, he groomed his own. His staff today consists of three former Duke captains: Johnny Dawkins — the program's all-time

> **"**
> I'm sure he felt extremely guilty about what happened in '95. He wanted to reestablish himself and reestablish the program.
>
> — VCU COACH JEFF CAPEL ON MIKE KRZYZEWSKI

leading scorer — Collins and Wojciechowski.

After the '95 season, Krzyzewski invited Collins and Capel to his house and made it clear that he would be different in the future, but Duke would again be Duke.

"He talked to us about how his commitment now was first to his family and then his team," Capel said. "You could kind of get a sense of it. We had maybe been insulated from that, but you saw a different look in his eye, almost like he felt like he had to prove himself all over again. ... I'm sure he felt extremely guilty about what happened in '95. He wanted to reestablish himself and reestablish the program."

Krzyzewski did it by adding the toughness that had been absent in '95. His next recruiting class, which arrived on campus in fall 1996, included Chris Carrawell, who grew up on the tough streets of St. Louis, and Nate James, son of a Marine sergeant. That fall, Duke's uniforms went from inoffensive royal blue to trendy black.

Gaudet moves on

While Krzyzewski was rebuilding, Gaudet had a career to consider. He spent a year teaching classes at Duke while continuing to work at basketball clinics and camps. In fall 1996, he was at a clinic in Korea when his wife called to relay an offer to become an assistant men's coach at Vanderbilt. Gaudet wasn't interested.

On the endless journey home via Japan and Chicago, Gaudet changed his mind. Coaching had not lost its appeal.

"I really enjoyed teaching in the classroom, and I thought the students really liked it," he said. "The coaching class was a very popular

course, and I taught some skills classes, too. In the end, it was about getting back on the floor and doing what I felt I did best."

In 1999, he switched from the men's to the women's team at Vandy, then moved with Jim Foster to OSU in 2002. Earlier this month, he was reassigned from assistant coach to video coordinator.

Though the four wins and 15 losses under Gaudet in 1995 were removed from Krzyzewski's coaching record, Duke does not list Gaudet among its head basketball coaches. Nor does Gaudet appear among the 19 former coaches and players included in Krzyzewski's "coaching tree" even though Krzyzewski once referred to him as "my main guy."

His departure from Duke basketball, only a decade past now, feels like much longer. "It just seems like a career ago," Gaudet said.

Lessons learned

Krzyzewski, meanwhile, has learned not to take winning for granted. Ten years after his health and his program crumbled, three trips to the Final Four and another national title later, he applied the lessons of 1995 to find success in 2005 after two key players jumped to the NBA.

Knowing strong legs would be essential, he insisted on the toughest offseason conditioning program of any Duke team. He

softened the schedule — Duke played only home and neutral-site games until the ACC season began in January — but approached every game as a must-win.

He simplified the offense and issued more instructions from the bench. He decided to apply less defensive pressure and steer more shots to Shelden Williams.

"There were a lot of question marks coming in, and he took it upon himself to make sure we went in the right direction," Duke's JJ Redick said.

Duke, picked to finish fourth in the ACC, won the title. After losing to Michigan State in the NCAA regional semifinals, Krzyzewski's disappointment with the loss clearly was tempered by an appreciation for the achievement.

"It's one of the greatest accomplishments I've had in coaching, for this group to finish up ACC champs and get a No. 1 seed," he said. "Believe me, it's a heck of a thing."

Duke's success last season — and promise for the next — remains a product of the changes made after the 1995 season. The legacy of that season lives on in the minds of Krzyzewski and Collins and Wojciechowski, who are determined never to repeat it.

Pete Gaudet, though, still is trying to forget.

"Good things are still happening," he said. "It's a blip for me. I don't really address it."

LEFT: Duke coach Mike Krzyzewski, returning from a back injury, talks with players during the first practice of the season, October 1995. NEWS & OBSERVER FILE PHOTO

Mike Krzyzewski
COACHING TREE

Jon Scheyer | **Mike Brey** | **Tommy Amaker** | **Steve Wojciechowski** | **Tim O'Toole** | **Nate James** | **Mike Dement**

Chris Collins | **Johnny Dawkins** | **Jeff Capel** | **Quin Snyder** | **David Henderson** | **Bob Bender** | **Mike Schrage**

RIGHT: From left, Duke basketball coaching staff Mike Krzyzewski, Johnny Dawkins, Steve Wojciechowski and Chris Collins applaud during the player introductions before the annual Blue-White Scrimmage at Cameron Indoor Stadium on Oct. 22, 2005. KEVIN SEIFERT / THE HERALD-SUN

OPPOSITE LEFT: Notre Dame coach Mike Brey, a former assistant under Mike Krzyzewski, complains about the lack of a foul call in Notre Dame's win over Charlotte in first-round NCAA action, March 13, 2002. SCOTT SHARPE / THE NEWS & OBSERVER

OPPOSITE TOP RIGHT: Duke head coach Mike Krzyzewski with former player and University of Washington head coach Bob Bender inside Cameron Indoor Stadium, 1998. Bender brought his team to Cameron Indoor to practice before an NCAA tournament being played in Greensboro, N.C. ROBERT WILLETT / THE NEWS & OBSERVER

OPPOSITE BOTTOM RIGHT: From left, Duke assistant coach Jon Scheyer, head coach Mike Krzyzewski and associate head coach Jeff Capel watch during the Blue Devils' 72-61 victory over Elon at the Greensboro Coliseum in Greenboro, N.C., Dec. 21, 2016. CHUCK LIDDY / THE NEWS & OBSERVER

30 years of camping at Krzyzewskiville

BY ANDREW CARTER, THE NEWS & OBSERVER • PUBLISHED MARCH 5, 2016

DURHAM, N.C. — Greg Esses still had the sleeping bag, the one he used 30 years ago when he spent two nights outside of Cameron Indoor Stadium before Duke played against North Carolina.

Not long ago, Esses gave that sleeping bag to his son.

Cameron Esses, a Duke freshman who shares his name with the building where Duke plays its home games, needed it for his first winter in Krzyzewskiville, the camp his father helped found in 1986. The sleeping bag, the younger Esses reported to his father, is the warmest in his 12-person tent.

"I was like, 'Your old man knows what he's doing,'" the elder Esses, a retired Air Force engineer, said during a phone interview earlier this week.

It was a Thursday, a few days before No. 1 Duke's game against UNC on March 2, 1986, Esses said, when "a ton of people showed up and started camping out" for seats to the game. He was among them.

Somebody scrawled a note on a piece of wood near the line of tents: "Don't even think about cutting this line. We've been here since Thursday. We'll kill you."

There was another sign not far away — small and simple, the words in big capital letters:

"KRZYZEWSKIVILLE POPULATION 3000+"

And so it began. Krzyzewskiville — one word now, no hyphen — turns 30 this weekend with the latest Duke-UNC game at Cameron Indoor Stadium. Back then it was small-time, named after a young Duke coach Mike Krzyzewski, then in his sixth season.

Now Krzyzewskiville is synonymous with Duke basketball — a living, breathing community that includes 100 tents, more than 1,000 students and about 30 line monitors who control the chaos.

"Seeing how it's all evolved and seeing what it is now — it is just a huge thing," said Wendy Burr, a senior who is one of Krzyzewskiville's two head line monitors. Burr grew up attending Duke games with her parents, both alums, and so she has seen Krzyzewskiville evolve over the years.

The Krzyzewskiville of today doesn't resemble what it was when it began. It grew, quickly, and soon students weren't camping out a couple of days before the UNC game but a couple of weeks before it instead. And that turned into four weeks, and then five, and with the increased time came increased regulation.

"I think that would be the reaction at this point if someone cut us in line," Jake Wirfel, a junior who is majoring in mechanical engineering, said on Thursday.

He and 11 others — Krzyzewskiville inhabitants can camp in groups as large as 12 — set up their tent on Jan. 17, 48 days before Duke's game against UNC. That was the earliest anyone could set up camp.

Last year Wirfel's group was in tent No. 2, which meant they were among the first people inside Cameron on the night of the UNC game. It was good but not good enough. So last April they began planning to be first in line.

OPPOSITE: Basketball inside Cameron Indoor Stadium and basketball outside Cameron Indoor Stadium as the Crazies play ball on portable baskets set up in front of the tent city called "Krzyzewskiville" on the campus of Duke University, March 3, 2016. CHUCK LIDDY / THE NEWS & OBSERVER

"We named our group chat 'Tent One or Die,'" said Haley Amster, a sophomore philosophy major who is in Wirfel's group. "So we were pretty set on being tent one."

It's not as simple as merely showing up first. Line order is largely determined by a point system that rewards attendance at other Duke sporting events. A Duke basketball trivia test also plays a role.

Wirfel and his group members haven't spent all 40-plus nights in their tent. Camping at Krzyzewskiville is divided into three periods: Black Tenting, Blue Tenting and White Tenting.

In Black Tenting, 10 members of a 12-person group are required to spend the night in tent. Then the requirement is six people and then, a couple weeks before the game, two people in each group must spend the night outdoors.

Throughout, at least one person is required to be with the tent at all times — grace periods excluded.

"The average person did 23 nights in the tent and a total of 73 day hours," said Quinn Hosler, a senior in Wirfel's group who organizes the tent schedule. "I think the max person did 26 and the minimum was at 19 nights."

It's a lot more than the two nights Esses spent in a tent 30 years ago. He sometimes bemoans what Krzyzewskiville has become. It used to be more organic.

"The bureaucracy now is just kind of crazy for all of it," he said. "It takes the fun out of it a little bit."

In the days before a game against UNC, the atmosphere in Krzyzewskiville is always festive, energetic, alive. It's not always that way in the weeks before that, though. Esses, one of the founding members of Krzyzewskiville, and Burr, the head line monitor, acknowledge a culture change at Duke over the years.

"Just with the academic pressures that have changed, I think Duke has become a much more academic school," Burr said. "Not that it wasn't before. And I think you can kind of see that, and parallel to basketball (interest has) dropped off a little bit."

The environment won't be in question on Saturday night, though. The atmosphere in and around Cameron Indoor Stadium will be electric in the hours before the game, as it always is when UNC visits, and the body-painting will commence two or three or four hours before tip-off.

In its early years, Krzyzewskiville was rustic. It is still, in some ways, but not like it was when Esses showed up two days before that 1986 UNC game and ran an extension cord to his tent from a window on the second floor of Cameron Indoor Stadium.

"I don't want to come off as, 'Oh we were so much better in the olden days,'" Esses said.

Yet in some ways, he feels that way. There was less structure, maybe some more fun, but far fewer nights outdoors.

"It's crazy," Cameron Esses, experiencing Krzyzewskiville for the first time, said of the differences between now and 30 years ago. "I'm having to do more than he ever had to do."

Seeing how it's all evolved and seeing what it is now — it is just a huge thing.

— WENDY BURR,
KRZYZEWSKIVILLE HEAD LINE MONITOR

ABOVE: Duke sophomore Jason Oettinger shoots photos of the snow in Krzyzewskiville before the Duke-Georgia Tech contest in Durham, N.C., on Jan. 17, 2013. CHUCK LIDDY / THE NEWS & OBSERVER

ABOVE LEFT: Spencer Davidson, a 19-year-old Duke University sophomore and a "Cameron Crazy," stays warm in an Ostrich Pillow Hat, Feb. 6, 2015. He and some friends were in the walk-up line for the Duke vs. Notre Dame game outside Cameron Indoor Stadium, also known as Krzyzewskiville. They were bracing for a chilly night after getting their spots in line earlier in the day. By getting in the line early they were guaranteed seats at center court for the 1 p.m. game. CHUCK LIDDY / THE NEWS & OBSERVER

OPPOSITE: "Cameron Crazy" Curtis Asbury cheers on the Blue Devils as they warm up before their game against Maryland at Cameron Indoor Stadium, Jan. 17, 2002. SCOTT SHARPE / THE NEWS & OBSERVER

LEFT: Dick Vitale, left, takes a quick break with Jonathan Roth, sophomore, at the tent city known as Krzyzewskiville, the day before the last home game against UNC on March 4. Roth had been camping out for a seat at the game since Feb. 16. COREY LOWENSTEIN / THE NEWS & OBSERVER

Duke nets third title

BY BARRY SVRLUGA, THE NEWS & OBSERVER • PUBLISHED APRIL 3, 2001

MINNEAPOLIS — They drew it up this way, you know. Just like this. Practice. Prepare. Play.

Win. Win again. Win some more.

Bring home the national championship.

So it was Monday night. Duke, for much of the season the best college basketball team in the land, ended it as such at the Metrodome. There, the Blue Devils beat Arizona, 82-72, to win the NCAA title, Duke's third overall, its first since 1992, when one of the best ACC teams ever won in this very building.

It was right there that Duke's Shane Battier — who has heard every conceivable compliment, earned every conceivable honor during his four years in Durham — crouched down in the waning moments, alone among the 45,994 on hand, whispering to himself, his career finally as complete as it could be.

Moments later, with 18 points, 11 rebounds, six assists and two blocks in the bag, the Final Four's Most Outstanding Player award became the final honor of his college career.

"It's complete," said Battier, who played in his 131st victory, tying him with Kentucky's Wayne Turner for the most ever. "All that's left for me is to ride off into the sunset on a white horse."

When Battier hops on that horse's back — to the NBA, or eventually to some governor's mansion — he will leave behind Duke coach Mike Krzyzewski, who overhauled these Blue Devils when center Carlos Boozer was injured late in the year. As much as the win completed Battier's career, it also put Krzyzewski square in the middle of an elite class, those coaches with three or more national championships.

Krzyzewski — who 21 years ago came to Duke unproven and unknown — joined UCLA's John Wooden (10), Kentucky's Adolph Rupp (4) and the man who coached Krzyzewski at Army, Indiana's Bobby Knight (3), as the only men to win more than two titles.

Those will do just fine for leading men. But for Duke (35-4) to oust the inspired and inspiring Wildcats (28-8) — who came into the tournament still filled with anguish over the New Year's Day death of coach Lute Olson's wife, Bobbi — there had to be more.

How about 21 points from sophomore Mike Dunleavy, 18 of them after Duke led by just two at halftime? Or a gutsy-if-not-glowing performance from point guard Jason Williams. Laden with foul trouble, limited to just 29 minutes, Williams' 16 points included a devastating 3-pointer with 1:44 left, a bucket that gave the Blue Devils an 80-72 advantage. Then, a dozen points and a dozen rebounds from Boozer, without whom the Devils likely don't win the title.

It was all needed. This matchup of the nation's two best teams may not have been as pretty as some would have liked. But the Devils will take it.

"Being so young, we showed toughness," Krzyzewski said. "We just did tough things, and I think we're deserving of it."

They deserved it during two spurts in the second half. Start with a two-point game, Duke up 39-37. That's when Dunleavy — who, in the first game-and-a-half of the Final Four, had scored just seven total points — arrived. How? Try three 3-pointers in a 45-second span, the bulk of a 10-2 Duke run that provided a 50-39 advantage.

Arizona, naturally, came back. And center Loren Woods helped them do it.

Woods, the 7-foot-1 enigma of a transfer

OPPOSITE: Duke's Shane Battier, right, shares a moment with Jason Williams (holding the NCAA championship trophy) as coach Mike Krzyzewski looks on after the Blue Devils' 82-72 NCAA championship win over Arizona, April 2, 2001. Casey Sanders is in the middle. CHUCK LIDDY / THE NEWS & OBSERVER

The Cameron Crazies put their arms up during a Duke foul shot at Cameron Indoor Stadium on Jan. 24, 2001, as Duke played Wake Forest. KEVIN SEIFERT / THE HERALD-SUN

from Wake Forest, led everybody with 22 points. He added 11 rebounds and four blocks, his best game at the right time.

"This was a huge game," Olson said. "And he came out and gave it a huge performance."

Then that next Duke run, and more from Dunleavy. He scored nine more points in a 14-4 surge that pushed the lead back to 61-51 with 10:07 to play.

Then, a pivotal point, it seemed. Williams — who had averaged 27.6 points in the NCAA tourney — picked up his fourth foul, a hack of Jason Gardner in the lane. 9:23 remained. Williams had to go to the bench.

If Arizona were to make a run, it seemed it would come now. It did.

Krzyzewski had to take a gamble and reinsert Williams with 6:13 remaining. Still, Richard Jefferson — who scored 19 points and hit 4 of his 8 3-pointers, while the rest of the Wildcats were 0-for-16 — nailed a 3. With 4:44 remaining, the Cats had clawed back, 71-68.

"We didn't want to go away," Jefferson said. "We were here to win."

And for a time, either team could have. Twice, it looked like Williams might foul out. But even with Olson raging on the sideline, there were no whistles.

"There are going to be calls that are going to be made," Olson said. "I frankly thought Jason Williams was fouled out twice."

Afterward, no one was arguing that any championship had been determined by a call or a non-call. The issue pushed aside, they played.

So with the lead at three, Battier won the championship. He followed up a Boozer miss with a jam filled with NBA panache. Eyes widened further on a twisting tip-in to make it 75-70.

"I don't see how he can explain that," Krzyzewski said. "I think his will to win, his will to keep us ahead ... he had an out-of-body experience or something."

Half a minute later, Jefferson hit what would be Arizona's last basket — a floater in the lane. It was then that Battier nearly gave Blue Devil fans their own out-of-body experience. A cut to the basket. A feed from Williams. A baseline, windmill, style-equals-substance stuff. With 2:30 left, it was 77-72.

Add Williams' 3-pointer— which came after he had missed 9 of his first 10 bombs — and the lead was insurmountable. As the clock ticked down, Battier realized what he had accomplished, the deed the Devils had done.

"I'm a firm believer in guardian angels," Battier said. "A couple of moments down the stretch, I believe my two angels were helping me."

Angels? That sounds good to Krzyzewski. With everything this team had accomplished, the title all sealed up, there seemed to be just one thing left for Battier to do.

"Can you do a favor for us?" Krzyzewski asked, looking at his senior. "Now that you're through playing, can you leave those guys behind?"

Duke 82, Arizona 72

PLAYER	MP	FG	FGA	FG%	2P	2PA	2P%	3P	3PA	3P%	FT	FTA	FT%	ORB	DRB	TRB	AST	STL	BLK	TOV	PF	PTS
Shane Battier	40	7	14	.500	6	9	.667	1	5	.200	3	6	.500	4	7	11	6	0	2	0	1	18
Chris Duhon	39	3	5	.600	2	4	.500	1	1	1.000	2	3	.667	1	3	4	6	0	0	1	2	9
Mike Dunleavy	32	8	17	.471	3	8	.375	5	9	.556	0	1	.000	2	1	3	0	0	0	0	3	21
Jay Williams	29	5	15	.333	3	4	.750	2	11	.182	4	6	.667	0	3	3	4	3	0	6	4	16
Casey Sanders	10	0	1	.000	0	1	.000	0	0		0	0		0	2	2	1	1	0	0	1	0
Carlos Boozer	30	5	9	.556	5	9	.556	0	0		2	3	.667	1	11	12	1	0	2	2	3	12
Nate James	20	2	3	.667	2	2	1.000	0	1	.000	2	3	.667	1	2	3	0	1	1	2	3	6
TOTAL	200	30	64	.469	21	37	.568	9	27	.333	13	22	.591	9	29	38	18	5	5	11	17	82

ABOVE: Duke point guard Jason Williams celebrates Duke's 98-96 overtime victory against Maryland in 2001. ROBERT WILLETT / THE NEWS & OBSERVER

RIGHT: Shane Battier urges his teammates to come together and rise to a higher level of play, Feb. 28, 2001. SCOTT LEWIS / THE NEWS & OBSERVER

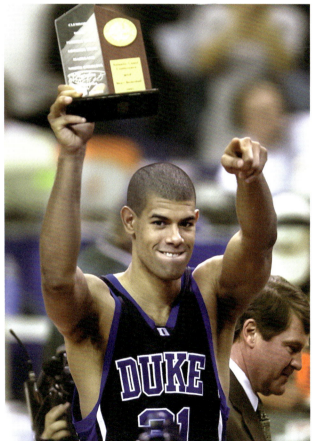

LEFT: Casey Sanders grins with his piece of the net after the Duke Blue Devils defeated the University of North Carolina 79-53 in the ACC championship game at the Georgia Dome in Atlanta, March 11, 2001. This was the 10th time that Duke and UNC had met in the ACC tournament's final game. Duke had won the previous two titles, and would be the first team to win three consecutive titles since UNC did from 1967–69. SCOTT LEWIS / THE NEWS & OBSERVER

BELOW: Shane Battier points to the crowd after receiving the ACC tournament MVP award where he led the Duke Blue Devils to a solid victory over the University of North Carolina, 79-53, in the ACC championship game at the Georgia Dome in Atlanta on March 11, 2001. SCOTT LEWIS / THE NEWS & OBSERVER

ABOVE: Duke forward Shane Battier drives the basket against tough defense by Maryland's Tahj Holden and Mike Mardesich, right, in the first half of their Final Four game, March 31, 2001, in the Metrodome in Minneapolis. CHUCK LIDDY / THE NEWS & OBSERVER

RIGHT: A frustrated Duke coach Mike Krzyzewski during the first half of their Final Four game against Maryland, March 31, 2001, in the Metrodome. CHUCK LIDDY / THE NEWS & OBSERVER

OPPOSITE: Duke center Casey Sanders looks up at the scoreboard as the Maryland lead grows in the first half of their Final Four game against Maryland, March 31, 2001. The Duke coaching staff looks on at right. CHUCK LIDDY / THE NEWS & OBSERVER

ABOVE: Duke coach Mike Krzyzewski hugs players Jason Williams and Shane Battier after Duke's come-from-behind win over Maryland, March 31, 2001, in the Metrodome. CHUCK LIDDY / THE NEWS & OBSERVER

RIGHT: Duke forward Carlos Boozer plays tough defense on Maryland's Lonny Baxter during their Final Four game, March 31, 2001, at the Metrodome in Minneapolis. CHUCK LIDDY / THE NEWS & OBSERVER

ABOVE: Duke center Casey Sanders dunks over Maryland's Tahj Holden in first-half action of their Final Four game, March 31, 2001, in the Metrodome. CHUCK LIDDY / THE NEWS & OBSERVER

LEFT: Duke guard Chris Duhon (21) shoots over some backward defense by Maryland's Steve Blake during the second half of their Final Four game, March 31, 2001, in the Metrodome. CHUCK LIDDY / THE NEWS & OBSERVER

ABOVE: Emily Krolak, left, and Stephanie McCray celebrate as Duke beats Maryland on March 31, 2001. The two Duke freshmen were watching the game remotely at Cameron Indoor Stadium. BILL WILLCOX / THE HERALD-SUN

RIGHT: Duke guard Jason Williams pushes the ball up the floor against Maryland in their Final Four game, March 31, 2001, in the Metrodome in Minneapolis. CHUCK LIDDY / THE NEWS & OBSERVER

Duke coach Mike Krzyzewski gives instruction to his players early in second-half action of the NCAA championship game, April 2, 2001, in the Metrodome. CHUCK LIDDY / THE NEWS & OBSERVER

ABOVE: Duke forward Mike Dunleavy drives past Arizona's Luke Walton in second-half action of the NCAA championship game, April 2, 2001, in the Metrodome.
CHUCK LIDDY / THE NEWS & OBSERVER

RIGHT: Duke's Jason Williams celebrates with coach Mike Krzyzewski, left, and other players after the Blue Devils 82-72 NCAA championship win over Arizona.
CHUCK LIDDY / THE NEWS & OBSERVER

Mike Krzyzewski gets a family hug from wife Mickie, left, and daughters Jamie, middle, and Lindy after the Blue Devils' NCAA championship win, April 2, 2001, in the Metrodome. CHUCK LIDDY / THE NEWS & OBSERVER

Shane Battier

Years at Duke: 1997–01
NBA Draft pick: No. 6
Team: Vancouver Grizzlies

Why his Duke jersey is retired

If anyone Mike Krzyzewski coached at Duke could challenge Shelden Williams as the most dominant man in the post, it was Shane Battier. As a three-time national defensive player of the year, he intimidated guards and forwards alike in the lane.

His 254 blocked shots rank third in Duke history and his 887 rebounds rank 13th.

But what made Battier stand out more was his ability to step out and shoot from outside. He made 246 3-pointers in his career (8th in Blue Devils history) at a .416 clip (5th).

His jersey was retired Feb. 21, 2001.

Duke stats and achievements

- Averaged 19.3 points and 7.3 rebounds as a senior
- National College Player of the Year (2001)
- National Defensive Player of the Year (1999, 2000, 2001)
- National champion (2001)
- Final Four Most Outstanding Player (2001)
- Consensus first-team All-American (2001)

RIGHT: Duke's Shane Battier blows the crowd a kiss after cutting down the net following the Blue Devils' 82-72 NCAA championship win over Arizona, April 2, 2001. CHUCK LIDDY / THE NEWS & OBSERVER

ABOVE: Shane Battier, left, and Jason Williams await their turn to go up on the winner's platform after the Blue Devils crushed the Tar Heels, March 11, 2003. CHUCK LIDDY / THE NEWS & OBSERVER

ABOVE LEFT: Duke's Nate James, left, congratulates Shane Battier (31) on drawing a foul and getting the two points from a layup during a game at Cameron Indoor Stadium. Battier, who was voted National Player of the Year by fellow players, garnered as much respect from his teammates as he did the legions of fans who followed his Blue Devil tenure. SCOTT LEWIS / THE NEWS & OBSERVER

LEFT: Duke's Chris Burgess wraps his arms around fellow freshmen Elton Brand, William Avery and Shane Battier, the nation's top-rated recruiting class. JIM BOUNDS / THE NEWS & OBSERVER

Jay Williams

Years at Duke: 1999–02
NBA Draft pick: No. 2
Team: Chicago Bulls

Why his Duke jersey is retired

At his best, Williams was practically unguardable in college. He could punish a defense from the perimeter with his shooting, or break it apart with his penetration and quickness. Along with Shane Battier and Mike Dunleavy (and Carlos Boozer and Chris Duhon), Williams led Duke to the 2001 national title and earned national player of the year honors the next season, as a junior.

He's also remembered for his role in the greatest comeback of the Coach K era — the victory at Maryland in 2001 when Duke erased a 12-point deficit in the final 65 seconds of regulation.

His jersey was retired Feb. 5, 2003.

Duke stats and achievements

- Averaged better than 21 points per game as a sophomore and junior
- Had a career average of 19.3 points and 6 assists in his three seasons
- National champion (2001)
- National Player of the Year (2002)
- Consensus first-team All-American (2001, 2002)

RIGHT: Front to back: Duke players Nate James, Jason Williams and Mike Dunleavy attempt to make their way through the crowd after practice in the Greensboro Coliseum, March 14, 2001. CHUCK LIDDY / THE NEWS & OBSERVER

ABOVE: Jason Williams attempts to block the shot of Notre Dame's David Graves during second-half action as Duke advances to the South region winning 84-77, March 16, 2002. CHUCK LIDDY / THE NEWS & OBSERVER

ABOVE LEFT: Duke's Jason Williams celebrates while cutting down the game net following Duke's 2002 ACC tournament championship game win over N.C. State. CHUCK LIDDY / THE NEWS & OBSERVER

LEFT: From left, Duke starters Mike Dunleavy, Jason Williams, Dahntay Jones, Carlos Boozer and Chris Duhon hold up the 2002 ACC championship trophy after beating State 91-61. CHUCK LIDDY / THE NEWS & OBSERVER

JJ Redick

Years at Duke: 2002–06
NBA Draft pick: No. 11
Team: Orlando Magic

Why his Duke jersey is retired

The 964 points Redick scored during his senior season in 2005–06 are the most of any player in Duke history, and more than 100 more than RJ Barrett, who ranks second in the Blue Devils' single-season records.

The only thing he didn't accomplish as a Blue Devil was a national championship, losing to Connecticut in the 2004 Final Four. Redick played 16 NBA seasons before retiring in 2021.

His jersey was retired Feb. 4, 2007, a week after teammate Shelden Williams.

Duke stats and achievements

- Averaged 26.8 points and 2.6 assists per game as a senior
- Career scoring average of 19.9 points
- Made a program-record 457 3-pointers in his career
- Consensus first-team All-American (2005, 2006)
- Consensus National Player of the Year (2006)
- ACC tournament champion (2003, 2005, 2006)

RIGHT: Duke shooting guard JJ Redick and Mike Krzyzewski celebrate in the last seconds of a 81-68 victory over N.C. State at Cameron Indoor Stadium at Duke University. ETHAN HYMAN / THE NEWS & OBSERVER

ABOVE: Duke's JJ Redick and Shelden Williams hold onto each other as they leave the court at Cassell Coliseum on the Virginia Tech campus in Blacksburg, Va., Jan. 26, 2006. Redick and Williams had 24 points each in the Blue Devils' 80-67 victory. CHUCK LIDDY / THE NEWS & OBSERVER

LEFT: Duke guard JJ Redick lets out a "Woooo!" as he's helped to his feet by teammates Greg Paulus and Shelden Williams after a hard foul in the second half of their battle against George Washington at the Greensboro Coliseum on March 18, 2006, during the second round of the NCAA tournament. Redick led the Blue Devils with 20 points as they beat the Colonials 74-61, advancing to the Atlanta Regional. CHUCK LIDDY / THE NEWS & OBSERVER

Shelden Williams

Years at Duke: 2002–06
NBA Draft pick: No. 5
Team: Atlanta Hawks

Why his Duke jersey is retired

Perhaps no post player in Duke history was more dominant than Shelden Williams — and that's saying a lot. Williams holds the program record for career rebounds with 1,262, 144 of which came in the NCAA tournament. His 422 career blocks are also a program record.

His 18 rebounds against Southern in 2006 are tied for the Duke record in an NCAA tournament game.

His jersey was retired Jan. 28, 2007, a week before teammate JJ Redick.

Duke stats and achievements

- Averaged 18.8 points and 10.7 rebounds as a senior
- Scored 1,928 points in his college career.
- National Defensive Player of the Year (2005, 2006)
- ACC Player of the Year (2005, 2006)
- ACC tournament champion (2003, 2005, 2006)

RIGHT: Former Duke basketball player Shelden Williams' jersey was retired during the halftime ceremony of the Duke vs. Boston College men's basketball game at Cameron Indoor Stadium on Jan. 28, 2007. MARK DOLEJS / THE HERALD-SUN

ABOVE: Duke forward Shelden Williams dunks on Seton Hall, Nov. 16, 2005, at Cameron Indoor Stadium. Duke won 93-40. BERNARD THOMAS / THE HERALD-SUN

ABOVE LEFT: From left, Duke head coach Mike Krzyzewski, JJ Redick, Shelden Williams, Sean Dockery, Lee Melchionni and DeMarcus Nelson listen to the U.S. national anthem before taking the floor for the annual Duke men's basketball Blue-White Scrimmage at Cameron Indoor Stadium on Oct. 22, 2005. KEVIN SEIFERT / THE HERALD-SUN

LEFT: Duke's Shelden Williams tries to marshal the team as UNC takes the lead in the second half at the Dean Smith Center, Feb. 7, 2006, in Chapel Hill, N.C. Duke came back to beat UNC 87-83. CHUCK LIDDY / THE NEWS & OBSERVER

Nail-biter gives Duke its fourth national championship

BY KEN TYSIAC, THE CHARLOTTE OBSERVER • PUBLISHED APRIL 6, 2010

INDIANAPOLIS — All season long, defense and rebounding were the buzzwords that carried Duke to the NCAA title game.

It was fitting, then, that one final defensive possession and a key rebound made the Blue Devils NCAA champions Monday night at Lucas Oil Stadium in a 61-59 thriller over Butler.

Trailing by one point, upset-minded Butler gave the ball to leading scorer Gordon Hayward. Guarded by Kyle Singler, he drove the right side of the lane but was cut off.

Hayward faded away to the baseline, where Duke's 7-foot-1 Brian Zoubek rushed out to contest the 10-foot jumper. Hayward had to adjust and lofted a high-arcing shot that rolled off the rim with 5 seconds remaining.

Zoubek rebounded for Duke with 3.6 seconds left. He made one free throw, then missed the next intentionally. A half-court heave by Hayward was long off the backcourt and the rim at the final horn.

Fireworks cracked and confetti fell, and Duke had its fourth NCAA title.

"We played a great game, they played a great game," said Duke coach Mike Krzyzewski while standing atop the podium with his team. "And it's hard for me to believe that we're the national champions."

Duke (35-5), the No. 1 seed out of the South Regional, stopped No. 5 seed Butler (33-5), a highly disciplined team from the mid-major Horizon League, just short of completing one of the most improbable championship runs ever.

"They gave it everything they have," Butler coach Brad Stevens said. "We just came up a bit short. ... I just told them that what they've done together will last a lot longer than one night, regardless of the outcome."

Singler, voted the tournament's Most Outstanding Player, led all scorers with 19 points. A junior who hasn't said yet whether he's returning to school or leaving for the NBA Draft, he was serenaded with a chant of "One more year!" by Duke's students as his award was announced.

Jon Scheyer scored 15 points and Nolan Smith 13 for the Blue Devils as the nation's top-scoring trio combined for 47 points in their final game together. Hayward and Shelvin Mack led Butler with 12 points apiece but combined to shoot just 7-for-25 from the field against a defense that made nearly every shot difficult.

"It means the world to us, especially this senior class," Duke senior forward Lance Thomas said. "We maxed out our season. ... To seal the deal at the end, I'm really at a loss for words."

Butler proved every bit as formidable as Krzyzewski had predicted the previous day. The game was billed as a classic meeting of a feisty, determined underdog against a highly skilled traditional power.

But Butler showed why it had won 25 in a row with a strong defensive performance that caused the Blue Devils fits. The Bulldogs backed off Thomas, Duke's least accomplished scorer, in order to clog the lane and pressure Scheyer, Singler and Smith.

OPPOSITE: Duke coach Mike Krzyzewski hugs senior forward Lance Thomas while Brian Zoubek clutches the school's fourth NCAA championship trophy following the 2010 title game in Indianapolis. CHUCK LIDDY / THE NEWS & OBSERVER

It was a brutal, half-court game that fit the styles of both teams and was tightly contested throughout. Although Duke led for most of the game, neither team ever led by more than six points.

Although its offense stalled, Duke defended aggressively and skillfully. The Blue Devils held Butler to 20-for-58 (34.5 percent) from the field and outrebounded the Bulldogs 20-11 in the second half to claim a 37-35 edge on the boards for the game.

Duke led 60-55 after two Smith free throws with 3:16 remaining but was held scoreless for the next 3:13. Howard scored a layup with 1:42 left and another with 54.8 seconds remaining to cut the Blue Devils' advantage to 60-59.

Singler missed a 15-foot jumper, and the rebound went out of bounds off Zoubek's leg with 33.7 seconds to go, giving Butler the ball. Zoubek deflected a Butler pass out of bounds with 13.6 seconds left, and the Bulldogs got the ball to Hayward for the pivotal shot that Zoubek's presence altered to help seal the win.

Smith celebrated the NCAA championship in the same city where his father, the late Derek Smith, helped Louisville defeat UCLA for the 1980 NCAA title. Singler claimed a championship that will have fans wondering if he will come back for another run.

And seniors Scheyer, Zoubek and Thomas completed their careers as champions who advanced deeper in the NCAA tournament in each of their four seasons at Duke.

"It's an unbelievable feeling," said Zoubek, who had eight points and 10 rebounds and bounced back from two foot surgeries early in his career to help make a title-winning play.

"You can see the product of the hard work I put in, and the hard work this team put in."

LEFT: Duke coach Mike Krzyzewski has a basketball tossed to him by a fan as he comes in from the Blue Devil's practice session at Lucas Oil Stadium. CHUCK LIDDY / THE NEWS & OBSERVER

OPPOSITE: Duke's Brian Zoubek, sitting, shows his passion as teammates Jon Scheyer, left, Lance Thomas (42) and Kyle Singler, right, celebrate a big play. CHUCK LIDDY / THE NEWS & OBSERVER

Duke 61, Butler 59

PLAYER	MP	FG	FGA	FG%	2P	2PA	2P%	3P	3PA	3P%	FT	FTA	FT%	ORB	DRB	TRB	AST	STL	BLK	TOV	PF	PTS
Kyle Singler	40	7	13	.538	4	7	.571	3	6	.500	2	2	1.000	1	8	9	2	1	2	2	1	19
Nolan Smith	40	5	15	.333	4	10	.400	1	5	.200	2	5	.400	1	2	3	4	0	0	3	0	13
Jon Scheyer	37	5	12	.417	4	7	.571	1	5	.200	4	5	.800	1	5	6	5	1	2	2	3	15
Lance Thomas	35	3	5	.600	3	5	.600	0	0		0	0		1	3	4	0	2	0	3	4	6
Brian Zoubek	31	3	4	.750	3	4	.750	0	0		2	4	.500	6	4	10	1	0	2	1	4	8
Miles Plumlee	9	0	2	.000	0	2	.000	0	0		0	0		1	2	3	0	1	1	1	2	0
Andre Dawkins	5	0	1	.000	0	0		0	1	.000	0	0		0	0	0	0	0	0	0	0	0
Mason Plumlee	3	0	0		0	0		0	0		0	0		0	1	1	0	0	0	0	0	0
TOTAL	**200**	**23**	**52**	**.442**	**18**	**35**	**.514**	**5**	**17**	**.294**	**10**	**16**	**.625**	**11**	**25**	**36**	**12**	**5**	**7**	**12**	**14**	**61**

Cameron Albin, right, a Duke sophomore, paints the face of friend Lewis Purcell, a freshman, before the national championship game between the Blue Devils and Butler at Lucas Oil Stadium in Indianapolis, April 5, 2010. CHUCK LIDDY / THE NEWS & OBSERVER

ABOVE: Cameron Crazies spell out Krzyzewski at a game against West Virginia in the national semifinals in Indianapolis. TED RICHARDSON / THE NEWS & OBSERVER

LEFT: Duke point guard Jon Scheyer drives around Devin Ebanks of West Virginia during the second half of the semifinals of the NCAA Men's Basketball Championship, April 3, 2010, at Lucas Oil Stadium in Indianapolis. CHUCK LIDDY / THE NEWS & OBSERVER

ABOVE: Duke's Kyle Singler, left, and Nolan Smith, celebrate as time runs out in the Blue Devils' NCAA Elite Eight victory over Baylor, 78-71. CHUCK LIDDY / THE NEWS & OBSERVER

RIGHT: Duke's Kyle Singler works against Butler's Avery Jukes in the NCAA title game on April 5, 2010. ETHAN HYMAN / THE NEWS & OBSERVER

ABOVE: Duke's Nolan Smith, who scored 13 points, goes up for a shot between Butler's Shelvin Mack (1) and Gordon Hayward (20). CHUCK LIDDY / THE NEWS & OBSERVER

LEFT: Duke point guard Nolan Smith drives around Butler's Shelvin Mack during the second half of Duke's victory. CHUCK LIDDY / THE NEWS & OBSERVER

ABOVE: Duke center Miles Plumlee, left, and Nolan Smith pressure Butler's Shawn Vanzant during the first half of the NCAA final at Lucas Oil Stadium. CHUCK LIDDY / THE NEWS & OBSERVER

OPPOSITE: Duke's Kyle Singler grabs a rebound in the second half. CHUCK LIDDY / THE NEWS & OBSERVER

ABOVE: Duke head coach Mike Krzyzewski holds up the net after defeating Butler 61-59 in the NCAA championship game at Lucas Oil Stadium in Indianapolis, April 5, 2010. CHUCK LIDDY / THE NEWS & OBSERVER

OPPOSITE: The Duke team watches a video of Final Four highlights after beating Butler 61-59 to win the NCAA championship in Indianapolis. CHUCK LIDDY / THE NEWS & OBSERVER

Tyus Jones, freshman Grayson Allen lead Duke to fifth title

BY LAURA KEELEY, THE NEWS & OBSERVER • PUBLISHED APRIL 6, 2015

INDIANAPOLIS — Mike Krzyzewski recruited one point guard for three years. And that player delivered him his fifth national title.

Duke beat Wisconsin 68-63 Monday night, the mission of the Blue Devils' freshmen complete.

It wasn't just Tyus Jones' talent that caught Krzyzewski's eye. It was his uncanny ability to stay poised with the game on the line, making the right decisions when most mortals would melt into a pool of nerves.

Jones finished with 23 points, and no shot was bigger than his 3-pointer with 1:24 left, putting Duke ahead 66-58. His two free throws with 34.9 seconds left once again gave Duke a cushion with a 68-63 lead.

Even after 38 games, Duke still had time for something new. Off nights from Quinn Cook, Justise Winslow and Jahlil Okafor didn't equal disaster thanks to perhaps the unlikeliest of heroes: Freshman Grayson Allen.

Allen didn't even play in Duke's 80-70 victory against the Badgers in December in Madison. And he had 18 points in the Blue Devils' first five tournament games. But he contributed 16 Monday night.

A lineup with Amile Jefferson at center — a move that happened for no more than a few minutes all season — and Allen as a primary scoring option was Duke's choice down the stretch.

Okafor was able to shake off his worst game of the season — limited to 22 minutes — in time to deliver a few daggers to the Badgers.

Saddled with four fouls, Okafor returned with 3:22 left and (finally) converted an inside shot, putting Duke ahead 61-58. And with the shot clock winding down on the other end, Frank Kaminsky was forced to throw up a prayer that did not hit the rim, giving Duke possession with 2:38 remaining.

The next possession featured Okafor pulling down an offensive rebound and converting on the second chance, putting the Blue Devils ahead with 63-58 with less than two minutes to play.

The game was fitting for the stage, with the first 20 minutes featuring 13 lead changes and a halftime score of 31-31. Just as it has been the case all season, Duke's freshmen were not rattled by the bright lights. And Cook, the senior captain, was locked in, twice diving into the corners of the Wisconsin end of the floor in attempts to save loose balls — quintessential Duke hustle plays revealing how badly he wanted to win his last game.

There were some tense moments for Duke in the first half. Okafor and Winslow both picked up two first-half fouls. Wisconsin had two, total, as a team. The disparity had Mike Krzyzewski and assistant Jeff Capel working the referees long into timeout periods.

Okafor picked up an offensive foul on Duke's third offensive possession, as Kaminsky drew the charge. Okafor was able to establish deep posting position on the senior and national player of the year, but Okafor had trouble finishing at the rim — more than he did in any other game this season.

The Blue Devils continued to play solid

OPPOSITE: Duke head coach Mike Krzyzewski hugs Duke's Tyus Jones after Duke's 68-63 victory over Wisconsin in the 2015 Division I Men's Basketball championship game at Lucas Oil Stadium in Indianapolis, April 6, 2015. CHUCK LIDDY / THE NEWS & OBSERVER

defense — outside of a stretch late in the first half during which Wisconsin scored on six of seven possessions with Winslow on the bench — but they had trouble finishing off possessions with rebounds. The Badgers collected eight offensive rebounds in the first half, turning them into 11 second-chance points — a significant factor into the 31-31 halftime draw.

Krzyzewski went to his short bench often in the first 20 minutes, and Allen contributed six first-half points. On one play in particular,

Krzyzewski called an isolation play for Allen — quite the display of faith in the last man off the bench.

He would certainly turn to him in the second, which started disastrously for Duke.

A quick 7-2 run by Wisconsin within the first 90 seconds prompted a quick Krzyzewski timeout. Jones had all six of Duke's points over the next three minutes, driving into the lane and drawing contact twice. Meanwhile, Okafor picked up his third foul with 16:50 left, Duke down 38-35.

It continued to get worse for Duke, as breakdowns on defensive switches started happening more often. A 6-0 Wisconsin run forced another Krzyzewski timeout with 13:17 left, Duke trailing 48-39. And then it was Allen who came to Duke's rescue.

Allen hit a 3 out of that timeout and then forced a turnover on the ensuing possession, diving to save a ball. Allen then proceeded to score Duke's next five points on drives to the basket, cutting the Wisconsin lead to 51-47.

Allen and Jones continued to pace Duke

offensively. Okafor, who struggled against Kaminsky all night, left the floor with his fourth foul with 9:18 remaining.

A Jones jump shot tied to game at 54 with 7:04 left — the first tie since halftime. An Allen drive about 90 seconds later gave Duke its first second-half lead. Kaminsky and Sam Dekker quickly answered with baskets.

But it was Jones again with the big shot, making a 3 as he fell to the floor in attempts to draw a whistle, putting Duke up 59-58 with 4:06 remaining.

Duke 68, Wisconsin 63

PLAYER	MP	FG	FGA	FG%	2P	2PA	2P%	3P	3PA	3P%	FT	FTA	FT%	ORB	DRB	TRB	AST	STL	BLK	TOV	PF	PTS
Tyus Jones	37	7	13	.538	5	10	.500	2	3	.667	7	7	1.000	0	5	5	1	0	0	1	1	23
Quinn Cook	35	3	8	.375	3	5	.600	0	3	.000	0	0		1	3	4	2	0	0	0	0	6
Justise Winslow	32	3	9	.333	2	7	.286	1	2	.500	4	7	.571	0	9	9	1	1	3	2	4	11
Matt Jones	23	0	1	.000	0	0		0	1	.000	0	0		1	2	3	0	1	0	0	0	0
Jahlil Okafor	22	5	9	.556	5	9	.556	0	0		0	1	.000	3	0	3	0	0	0	2	4	10
Grayson Allen	21	5	8	.625	4	6	.667	1	2	.500	5	5	1.000	0	2	2	0	1	0	0	0	16
Amile Jefferson	21	1	1	1.000	1	1	1.000	0	0		0	0		1	6	7	2	1	3	0	3	2
Marshall Plumlee	9	0	2	.000	0	2	.000	0	0		0	0		0	0	0	1	0	0	0	1	0
TOTAL	**200**	**24**	**51**	**.471**	**20**	**40**	**.500**	**4**	**11**	**.364**	**16**	**20**	**.800**	**6**	**27**	**33**	**7**	**4**	**6**	**5**	**13**	**68**

ABOVE: Duke coach Mike Krzyzewski reacts to a basket by his team late in the second half against Wisconsin on April 6, 2015, in Indianapolis. ROBERT WILLETT / THE NEWS & OBSERVER

RIGHT: Duke head coach Mike Krzyzewski, center, celebrates with assistant Jon Scheyer, left, and Nate James after Duke's 68-63 victory over Wisconsin in the 2015 Division I Men's Basketball championship, April 6, 2015. CHUCK LIDDY / THE NEWS & OBSERVER

LEFT: Duke head coach Mike Krzyzewski is excited during the second half of Duke's game against Wisconsin in the 2015 Division I Men's Basketball championship game at Lucas Oil Stadium in Indianapolis, April 6, 2015. ROBERT WILLETT / THE NEWS & OBSERVER

ABOVE: Duke head coach Mike Krzyzewski, right, talks with Grayson Allen, left, after Duke's 68-63 victory over Wisconsin in the 2015 Division I Men's Basketball championship game, April 6, 2015. CHUCK LIDDY / THE NEWS & OBSERVER

OPPOSITE: Duke head coach Mike Krzyzewski talks with his team after Duke's 68-63 victory over Wisconsin in the 2015 Division I Men's Basketball championship game, April 6, 2015. CHUCK LIDDY / THE NEWS & OBSERVER

RIGHT: Duke head coach Mike Krzyzewski celebrates after cutting down the net following Duke's 68-63 victory over Wisconsin in the 2015 Division I Men's Basketball championship game, April 6, 2015. CHUCK LIDDY / THE NEWS & OBSERVER

OPPOSITE: Coach Mike Krzyzewski, center, starts to dance during a welcome home celebration in Durham, N.C. The Duke Blue Devils basketball team returned as campus heroes, April 7, 2015, after winning the NCAA national championship in Indianapolis the night before against the Wisconsin Badgers. Students and fans packed Cameron Indoor Stadium to celebrate the team's fifth national championship. COREY LOWENSTEIN / THE NEWS & OBSERVER

'Amazing decision' opens right door for Krzyzewski, leads to Hall of Fame

BY NED BARNETT, THE NEWS & OBSERVER • PUBLISHED OCT. 6, 2001

SPRINGFIELD, Mass. — Decades after they sat together in the Polish kid's Chicago living room and talked about his basketball future, Bob Knight and Mike Krzyzewski sat together again Friday, this time on a stage at the Basketball Hall of Fame.

No matter how glowing Knight's promises were as he recruited Krzyzewski for Army in the mid-1960s, they were exceeded by what actually became of their getting together.

Knight, who went on to become a legend at Indiana, was inducted into the Hall of Fame in 1991. On Friday, he helped the kid from Chicago put on a Hall of Fame blazer and presented him for inclusion among the greatest in the game that James Naismith invented here.

The Duke coach, wearing his new jacket and an invisible mantle that will last as long as basketball is played, recalled how that first meeting between Knight and his family ended. "When [Knight] walked out, my dad said, 'Well, that's where you're going.' Though I didn't necessarily want to do that for a while, I followed [his] advice, and it's turned out to be an amazing decision."

Krzyzewski learned to coach as a point guard for West Point and later as an assistant to Knight at Indiana. Knight also pushed Krzyzewski as a candidate when the Duke head coaching job came open in 1980.

Thirty years after their first meeting, the two men have each won three NCAA national championships — totals exceeded only by John Wooden's 11 with UCLA and Adolph Rupp's four with Kentucky.

Also inducted Friday were Temple coach John Chaney, presented by former Georgetown coach John Thompson, and Moses Malone, a 12-time NBA All-Star who was presented by his former Philadelphia 76ers teammate, Julius Erving.

Although the ceremony focused attention on Krzyzewski's entire career — "I feel like I'm retiring, and I'm not," he said Thursday — his relationship with Knight, or rather his renewed relationship, drew the most comment. The two men reportedly have been estranged since the early 1990s when Krzyzewski's accomplishments, including Duke's 1992 Final Four defeat of Indiana, began to surpass Knight's reputation.

Krzyzewski, who must be presented by a member of the Hall of Fame, had called Knight in August and asked him to do the honors. The request apparently thawed their relationship. In a meeting with reporters after the jacket fitting, Knight and Krzyzewski sat side by side exchanging compliments.

Knight, a four-time National Coach of the

OPPOSITE: Duke men's basketball coach Mike Krzyzewski prepares for a news conference announcing his induction into the Naismith Memorial Basketball Hall of Fame, May 30, 2001. The announcement was on a teleconference with hall of fame officials in Springfield, Mass. The other two inductees in the 2001 class are Temple University coach John Chaney and former NBA great Moses Malone. SCOTT LEWIS / THE NEWS & OBSERVER

Year at Indiana, praised Krzyzewski's record and his success in having players who graduate and show strong character. "As I look at all the kids I've had and coached — and there have been an awful lot of good ones — I think Mike has really gone as far as a guy could conceivably go in what he's chosen to do," Knight said. "And that's secondary. The most important thing is that he's done everything right. He's done it the way it should be done."

Krzyzewski said Knight started him on the path to Springfield. "Everybody needs a start. I actually got two starts with him, one as a player and then one as an assistant coach," he said.

The Duke coach dismissed talk of the strained relationship with Knight. "For me, I've had a good relationship since that night that he came into my house," Krzyzewski said. "He's had a big bearing on who I am today. To share this day with him, as I will with my former and current players, is the right thing. It feels good to do that."

Krzyzewski also singled out the athletics director who hired him at Duke and resisted pressure to fire him when his team performed poorly during his first three years.

"The two dominant personalities and the smartest people that I've been associated with professionally are Coach Knight and my athletic director at Duke, Tom Butters," Krzyzewski said. "[Butters] let me have a certain amount of autonomy that a coach needs, but he was there for guidance and a little bit of encouragement at times."

Knight, his once trademark red Indiana sweater replaced by a color approaching a Carolina hue that he called "Cara-Knight Blue," seemed to make an effort to avoid the cutting comments that mark his solo news conferences. He wasn't entirely successful.

Krzyzewski said, "I don't think coaches get the support that they [once] did. I was 38-47 my first three years at Duke. If that was today, I might be writing columns."

Knight interjected, "Aspire to something higher than that."

Krzyzewski, still taking cues from his coach, added, "I was just saying if I was really down, coach, I might have just fallen into anything, something you could do without much education."

Once he started coaching college basketball, Krzyzewski said, he knew he had made the right choice. He has never looked elsewhere, even when the NBA came calling.

"I'm doing exactly what I want to do," he said. "I really respect the pro game, and I have a lot of friends and some players in the pros, but college basketball has really given me great fulfillment. I never really came close to doing anything else."

On Friday night, Krzyzewski was escorted to the podium at the Springfield Civic Center by his three daughters, Debbie, Lindy and Jamie. In front of a crowd of 3,200, the coach fought back emotion, his lips trembling and his eyes shining with tears. At the podium, he paused, swallowed and said, "Wow."

He compared his career to a train full of people and said, "Now my train is in Springfield."

At the close of his remarks, he called his wife, Mickie, to the podium and said, "You never accomplish all that you accomplish alone. My train has been full of great people. I can tell you this has been the best person on my train — and we're going to keep the train going."

I'm doing exactly
what I want to do.

— MIKE KRZYZEWSKI ON
COACHING COLLEGE BASKETBALL

LEFT: Duke basketball coach Mike Krzyzewski gets a hug from his daughter, Jamie, after a news conference announcing Krzyzewski being voted into the Basketball Hall of Fame, May 30, 2001, in Durham, N.C. KEVIN SEIFERT / THE HERALD-SUN

OPPOSITE: Duke men's basketball coach Mike Krzyzewski speaks about his family, his players and his career as a coach during a news conference announcing his induction into the Naismith Memorial Basketball Hall of Fame on May 30, 2001. SCOTT LEWIS / THE NEWS & OBSERVER

A 903rd win is just a win by any other name

BY LUKE DECOCK, THE NEWS & OBSERVER • PUBLISHED NOV. 16, 2011

NEW YORK — When Mike Krzyzewski won the first game of his coaching career, the player who would deliver him his 903rd was still almost 16 years away from being born.

Andre Dawkins was born on Sept. 19, 1991, years after Army beat Lehigh on Nov. 28, 1975, to inaugurate a coaching career that still rolls on 36 years later and when, on a Tuesday night at Madison Square Garden, Dawkins scored 26 points to help Duke to a 74-69 win over Michigan State that meant nothing and everything.

It moved Duke to 3-0 on the season, gave the Blue Devils a second quality win over an NCAA tournament-caliber team, and secured Krzyzewski's place in basketball history, not that he wasn't there already, in front of his own coach at Army, the man who until Tuesday night held the record with 902 wins, Bobby Knight.

When it was over, Krzyzewski shook hands with Michigan State coach Tom Izzo, then headed straight across the court to Knight, who was working as an analyst for ESPN.

Krzyzewski and Knight shared a prolonged embrace as his players donned "903" hats.

After a presentation at midcourt with NCAA president Mark Emmert, it was on to his wife Mickie, sitting behind the Duke bench, and then a huddle with his team before he was ushered off the court, with more celebration to come later in the night.

But, this 903rd win is just another win for a coach who has won hundreds.

It doesn't secure a 12th trip to the Final Four. It doesn't win a fifth national title.

It doesn't win another Olympic gold medal.

It doesn't set the bar, because Krzyzewski is nowhere near finished.

It's a nice nonconference win on a November night that gets the record out of the way so Krzyzewski can move on to the real business at hand: Getting a very young Duke team ready for ACC play, ready to win games like this in March and April when they matter for reasons that have nothing to do with the coach and how long he's been around.

And oh, how he's been around — long enough to watch his players become pros and broadcasters, and coaches. Many of them were at Madison Square Garden on Tuesday, and three of them even sat beside him on the Duke bench.

At this point in his career, with the record and the national titles and the Final Fours and the gold medal, it's fair to ask, what's next?

The answer, as always, is another game, another win, another step forward toward the goals that really matter — ACC championships, Final Fours and national titles.

He won't be happy with the way the Blue Devils played late, as a 20-point lead dwindled down to five.

After Duke couldn't get the ball inbounds with 13 seconds to play, Michigan State had a chance at a 3-pointer that could have further narrowed the gap — maybe even put win 903 in doubt.

It'll be a learning moment for Krzyzewski, and it's hard to imagine him complaining too

---

OPPOSITE: Duke head coach Mike Krzyzewski holds the game ball and is surrounded by players after he secured his 903rd career victory. Duke played Michigan State University at Madison Square Garden in New York City, Nov. 15, 2011. CHUCK LIDDY / THE NEWS & OBSERVER

loudly about that — his team won, and there's something to work on in practice this week, once the 903 hats have been cleared out of the locker room.

The record will continue to grow, but in the background, Krzyzewski will go back to work — still at work after more than three decades and 903 wins.

RIGHT: Duke forward Mason Plumlee (5) goes up to block a second-half shot by Michigan State center Derrick Nix (25). CHUCK LIDDY / THE NEWS & OBSERVER

ABOVE: Duke forward Miles Plumlee (21) rips a rebound from Michigan State's Travis Trice (20) and Adreian Payne (5) at Madison Square Garden in New York City, Nov. 15, 2011. CHUCK LIDDY / THE NEWS & OBSERVER

LEFT: Duke guard Seth Curry (30) upends MSU's Travis Trice (20) in the first half of play. Trice was called for the foul. CHUCK LIDDY / THE NEWS & OBSERVER

ABOVE: Fans hold up signs after Duke head coach Mike Krzyzewski breaks the all-time NCAA Division I record. Duke played Michigan State University at Madison Square Garden in New York City, Nov. 15, 2011. CHUCK LIDDY / THE NEWS & OBSERVER

ABOVE RIGHT: Duke head coach Mike Krzyzewski, right, is congratulated by assistant Chris Collins and Jeff Capel, left, as the buzzer sounds and he becomes the winningest NCAA Division I basketball coach of all time with 903 wins, Nov. 15, 2011. CHUCK LIDDY / THE NEWS & OBSERVER

OPPOSITE: Duke head coach Mike Krzyzewski, right, speaks with mentor and former NCAA Division I record holder Bobby Knight as Krzyzewski wins number 903 to become the winningest coach of all time. CHUCK LIDDY / THE NEWS & OBSERVER

RIGHT: Duke forward Marshall Plumlee (40) holds up a sign as Duke head coach Mike Krzyzewski accepts the game ball. CHUCK LIDDY / THE NEWS & OBSERVER

Dean Smith got the best of Coach K, then he got the best from him

BY ANDREW CARTER, THE NEWS & OBSERVER • PUBLISHED MARCH 5, 2022

There are moments, still, when Mike Krzyzewski walks into his top-floor office that overlooks part of Duke's campus and wonders, as he put it one day last summer, "How the hell did this happen?"

"No, really," he said.

He was surrounded by reminders of his life's work, in a building that didn't exist when he arrived in Durham 42 years ago. Now there was a Duke basketball museum on the first floor and here, five stories up, a museum of a different kind, one Krzyzewski personally curated.

Five large photographs of his teams celebrating five national championships hung high behind his desk. Old game balls and magazine covers lined the walls, along with honors from West Point and snapshots of his wife and daughters and grandchildren.

All around were odes to his most cherished people and moments, the things he loved, and for almost two hours he'd been reflecting upon some of them while attempting to keep a distance. The season was then months away and Krzyzewski insisted that once it began he'd stay in the present. There'd be no talk of the last of this or the last of that, he said. Even then, in mid-August, without a game to worry about or a practice to plan, he said he'd rather not look back.

Then he felt the pull of history.

"One more thing from me," Krzyzewski said, just as a long conversation wound down, and it was as if he had a secret to share. Perhaps he just wanted people to know that things could change, that he could change — that an old rival or nemesis could become something much more meaningful. His tone changed, too, as if he was even surprised at what he was about to say.

"Being in this area, with North Carolina State, but especially North Carolina, and our rivalry, relationship or whatever ... The friendship I eventually developed with Dean was kind of nuts."

It was an unprompted addendum to a long interview, and soon Krzyzewski was on his feet, walking to the other side of his office. He didn't fight the past now, memories of when he was much younger and attempting to build something in the shadow of what Dean Smith had built at North Carolina. Theirs was not an especially warm relationship in the beginning. Smith's UNC teams beat Duke again and again during Krzyzewski's early years. Sometimes Krzyzewski bristled.

"I needed to go through all that," he said, and he made his way to a wall where he'd hung photos of himself with some of his closest friends — one with Jim Boeheim; another of Krzyzewski and Jim Valvano, both young, in the prime of their lives. That was a long time ago now. And then above, in the

---

OPPOSITE: Duke basketball coach Mike Krzyzewski, center, and N.C. State basketball coach Jim Valvano listen as UNC coach Dean Smith talks with them before a preseason press conference in 1987. NEWS & OBSERVER FILE PHOTO

middle — "let me show you," Krzyzewski said, "this is a cool picture" — was one of Smith and Krzyzewski in Smith's later years.

They were sitting beside each other, suit jackets and ties, at a function at the North Carolina Sports Hall of Fame. They appeared to be sharing a laugh, or maybe only a smile. The scars of their old battles had faded away; one of the fiercest coaching rivalries in ACC history had become something more tender, something Krzyzewski still had difficulty articulating, years later.

In the photo, Smith and Krzyzewski looked like old friends. They'd become that, Krzyzewski said.

"And to me, that's like one of the hidden things in the history of our league," Krzyzewski said of his relationship with Smith, one that evolved into something meaningful, for both men, before Smith died in 2015. "Is how the hell could that happen?"

• • •

Krzyzewski will coach his final home game on Saturday. For 42 years he has made the short walk from the Duke locker room to the home bench on the opposite side of Cameron Indoor Stadium. It has become one of the most reliable constants in American sport, Krzyzewski's presence, and no one born after March 17, 1980, has known a world without Krzyzewski as the head coach at Duke.

The game Saturday will not only be the last one he coaches at Cameron Indoor Stadium, but also the last one he coaches in North Carolina, which hosts neither the ACC tournament nor an NCAA tournament site. And it might be the last one he coaches against North Carolina, the school, the one Krzyzewski has most often been measured against over the past four decades.

The UNC-Duke basketball rivalry has long needed no explanation. It simply exists, a product of the schools' shared history and tradition and often successful pursuit of the same things; a product of their proximity and the whole "separated by eight miles of pine trees and two shades of blue" dynamic that ESPN dramatized in the old promos leading into the broadcasts.

The rivalry has been what it is for so long that it's difficult to consider a time when it wasn't that way, though that time existed, too. When Krzyzewski arrived in Durham in 1980, Duke hadn't defeated UNC in Chapel Hill since 1966.

The Blue Devils had experienced national success — they'd been to three consecutive NCAA tournaments, including a regional final — during the previous three seasons under Bill Foster, but not sustained national success. The ACC was much smaller then, more regionally confined and perhaps more contentious, every coach fighting for the limited opportunity to break through the grind of the regular season and reach the NCAA tournament. Terry Holland had built something lasting at Virginia. So had Lefty Driesell at Maryland. Dean Smith was already a beloved figure in this state, even if he had yet to lead UNC to a national championship.

Smith was 49, and a refined and accomplished presence when Krzyzewski entered the league. Krzyzewski then was 33, and he looked a little nervous at his introductory press conference, smiling sheepishly and spelling his name for the reporters who didn't yet have a chance to know how to pronounce it. They coached against each other for the first time on Dec. 5, 1980, in the last year of the old Big Four Tournament in Greensboro.

"I'm worried about Duke," Smith told reporters before the game. "They've got a great young coach."

I'm worried about Duke. They've got a great young coach.

— DEAN SMITH ON MIKE KRZYZEWSKI
BEFORE THEIR FIRST MATCHUP IN 1980

Perhaps he was just being kind. Perhaps he really saw greatness in Krzyzewski, who arrived from Army relatively unknown. Either way, Smith led UNC to a close two-point victory in the Greensboro Coliseum, and Krzyzewski was 0-1 against Smith.

The teams met again about a month and a half later in Chapel Hill. Unlike their first game that season, this one counted in the conference standings.

These days, ESPN builds its college basketball television inventory around the two annual UNC-Duke games. They're always among the most watched of the season. But back then, in early 1981, Krzyzewski's first ACC regular-season game against UNC was not televised live. Locally, it aired on tape delay on WTVD at 10 p.m. The Tar Heels won by 15, and the headline in The News

& Observer the next morning said: "Heels crush Blue Devils."

Krzyzewski was 0-2 against Smith, but not for long. He guided the Blue Devils to a 66-65 overtime victory against UNC about a month later, in Krzyzewski's first game against UNC in Cameron Indoor Stadium. Down two at the end of regulation, with two seconds remaining, Krzyzewski drew up a play to get the ball to mid-court and then, after another timeout with one second left, he set up the play that sent it into overtime.

"Hectic, feverish, spine-tingling, nail-biting," went The N&O game story the next day.

It was considered then one of the great finishes in the history of the series.

Krzyzewski was 1-2 against Smith. And then: 1-3, and 1-4, and 1-5, and 1-6, and 1-7, and 1-8.

More than three years passed before Krzyzewski beat Smith and the Tar Heels again.

• • •

During that span, Smith won his first national championship in 1982. Valvano, who arrived at N.C. State the same year that Krzyzewski did at Duke, led the Wolfpack to that improbable national championship in 1983. That same March, meanwhile, some wondered whether Krzyzewski might be fired after an 11-17 finish.

Even amid the losing, Krzyzewski developed little taste for deferring to anybody, least of all Smith. Roy Williams, then a young assistant coach under Smith, sensed that from the beginning.

"Mike came in, and the first couple years

Duke coach Mike Krzyzewski, surrounded by former players, enters Cameron Indoor Stadium in Durham, N.C., for his final home game on March 5, 2022, played against North Carolina. ROBERT WILLETT / THE NEWS & OBSERVER

ABOVE: Duke head coach Mike Krzyzewski speaks to the crowd during a ceremony after the Blue Devils game against North Carolina at Cameron Indoor Stadium in Durham, N.C., March 5, 2022. ETHAN HYMAN / THE NEWS & OBSERVER

RIGHT: Duke coach Mike Krzyzewski is recognized in Cameron Indoor Stadium, surrounded by former players, prior to his final home game on March 5, 2022, in Durham, N.C. ROBERT WILLETT / THE NEWS & OBSERVER

were tough," he said recently. "And Mike needed to stand up to anybody and everybody. ... He had to make sure that people didn't think he was going to give in to anybody. And so he was very competitive. And Coach Smith was very competitive.

"And, you know, some of the things that people thought about or people saw or people heard, made it feel like it was a very adversarial relationship."

It was intense from the start. More than 40 years later, Williams can still see the final seconds of UNC's victory against Duke in the 1980 Big Four Tournament, in Krzyzewski's first game against the Tar Heels. Smith began walking toward Krzyzewski to shake his hand, Williams said, "but there were still a couple of seconds left."

Krzyzewski, as Williams remembers it, offered a terse response:

"The game's not over yet."

"And that irritated some people, too," Williams said. "But again, it's in competition. So it was something that made me realize that guy really is a competitive guy. And that was OK."

Williams became UNC's head coach in 2003 and spent 18 seasons going head-to-head against Krzyzewski, himself, until Williams retired last April. Their relationship was different because they were more peers, men of roughly the same ages and ones who established themselves throughout the 1980s and '90s.

Once in the early 1980s, Williams said, he took the junior varsity team he coached at UNC to Durham to play against Duke's JV team. Krzyzewski, fighting to build something in those years, had just wrapped up the varsity practice. Williams walked onto the court at Cameron Indoor Stadium and met Krzyzewski and the two shared a conversation in the quiet of an empty arena.

"They only had a (JV) team for a couple of years, but Mike and I are sitting there talking for 20 or 30 minutes while my guys are getting dressed," Williams said, "So we had some opportunities to do those kinds of things that Coach Smith and Mike did not have."

In those years, Smith and Krzyzewski knew each other only as obstacles to what the other wanted. Smith had established himself as one of the nation's great coaches, and his program could not be the best in the country if it was not the best in his own backyard. Krzyzewski, meanwhile, looked at everything Smith had created and spent years trying to build his own version of it.

"I never, like, wanted to copy him," Krzyzewski said, recalling what Vic Bubas told him when he arrived at Duke: "Don't look eight miles away. Respect eight miles away. You develop what you're going to do."

"And that was great advice," Krzyzewski said, though as a lot of good advice it was difficult to implement. How could Krzyzewski not look eight miles southwest, after all? In his early years, his frustration simmered, then erupted after a 78-73 defeat against UNC in Durham on Jan. 21, 1984.

The week before, the Duke student section received national criticism for its heckling of Herman Veal, a Maryland player who'd been accused of sexual assault. Then, during the UNC game, Krzyzewski became angered when Smith approached the scorer's table, twice, "to dispute developments," as a writer for the Durham Herald-Sun described it the next day.

"Both times he lingered and argued," the story went in the paper.

After a close loss, Krzyzewski chided reporters and called out Smith, which to many in North Carolina was something like sacrilege.

"When you come in here and start writing about Duke having no class, you better start getting your heads straight," Krzyzewski said then. "Because our students had class and our team had class."

He continued, taking a direct shot at Smith:

"There was not a person on our bench who was pointing at officials or banging on the scorers' table or having everybody running around on their bench. So let's get some things straight around here and quit the double standard that sometimes exists in this league. All right?"

Almost 40 years later, Krzyzewski recently considered those comments.

"Competitive bullshit," he said, but not without adding that "I needed to go through that," and "if you were me, you would feel the same way," and "there probably was" a double standard, and how now "they probably feel the same way with me" though Smith "probably had a better one than me," Krzyzewski said with a laugh.

"But no," he said. "It wasn't calculated. Spur of the moment. ... Then I got it. I got it.

"And that was really good. I'm so happy that I got it. Actually, we became friends."

• • •

The last time Krzyzewski and Smith coached against one another was exactly 25 years ago Wednesday. It was March 2, 1997. A match-up of top-10 teams in Chapel Hill. Ed Cota dribbled out the clock during the final seconds of the Tar Heels' 91-85 victory. Brent Musburger and Dick Vitale wrapped up their nationally televised broadcast on ABC.

Smith and Krzyzewski shook hands near midcourt. It was a brief exchange. Before it ended, their right hands still touching, Smith leaned in closer and placed his left hand on Krzyzewski's back, almost a half hug. Smith shared a quick word, moving in to speak into Krzyzewski's ear, and then the two men went their separate ways.

It was the last time, as head coaches, that their paths crossed on a basketball court. Nobody could have known then that it was Smith's final game inside the building named after him; that he'd lead the Tar Heels to one more Final Four before retiring about seven months later. And nobody could have known that Krzyzewski, then 50, had 25 more years of coaching in him.

Smith retired having won more games than anyone in the history of the sport. Krzyzewski will do the same whenever Duke's season ends. He has won five national championships. He has won 15 ACC tournament championships. He has won 1,196 games, more than enough for some of those victories to run together.

The losses are much fewer, and so they stand out more. And Krzyzewski lost against no coach more often than he lost against Dean Smith. Krzyzewski will retire with a winning record against UNC — he's 50-46, entering Saturday — but he was 14-24 against Smith, who often seemed so far ahead and out of reach during Krzyzewski's early years.

"When we went to Final Fours, and won, I knew him," Krzyzewski said. "I didn't know him until I did that. And he knew then that I knew him. And then I could appreciate his genius, just how damn good he was. And he recognized that, eventually, in me.

"And I love Dean Smith. And I respect the hell out of him."

In a way, Krzyzewski has become what Smith was, but "I don't want to say it that way," he said, "because nobody can be who he was." He understands the differences. Smith's legacy is clear beyond basketball, most notably as a Civil Rights advocate in the South when it was uncomfortable for a white man of prominence to take the stands that he did. They're different in personality and demeanor, and yet these dissimilar men, once fierce adversaries, eventually formed a bond.

"That's why his picture's up there," Krzyzewski said, and he shared a story he'd rarely shared before. It was the story the last time he spent time with Smith, when Smith was suffering from a dementia-like condition that robbed him of his mind and his memories.

"He only got so much," Krzyzewski said. "God bless him — you know, sad.

"But Linnea let us come over, and visit with him."

This was at the beach, on Figure Eight Island. Krzyzewski had rented a house there for his family, and by chance it so happened to be close to a house where the Smiths were staying.

"Serendipity," Linnea Smith, Dean's widow, said during a recent phone interview. She values her privacy and rarely speaks publicly, but she agreed to talk about this, about one final long meeting between two of the greatest coaches in American sports history, who did some of their most memorable work against one another.

Linnea could not remember the year, only that it was toward "the very end" of her husband's illness. Occasionally, she said, the family would take him to the beach. It was difficult, she said, because he was confined to a wheelchair and he had trouble eating and "he couldn't articulate much at all."

"You wondered how much he was processing of what was happening around him," she said. "But he would be in the wheelchair, and we'd take him out on the deck. And I think the beach and the surf was calming."

One day, after a chance encounter between the families, Krzyzewski asked Linnea if he and Mickie, his wife, could come over and spend time with Dean. At first, Linnea wasn't sure, she said, "Because I wasn't sure how helpful that would be." After some thought, Linnea, who'd long been friendly with Mickie and some of the other old coaches' wives, Pam Valvano included, agreed and invited the Krzyzewskis over.

She tried to prepare them for Dean's condition. Mike Krzyzewski wanted to visit him for a couple of reasons, but most of all to tell Dean Smith what Krzyzewski had known all along, even when they did not like each other very much. He wanted to tell him that, "I knew that there wouldn't be anybody ever like him."

"And I wanted to let him know that I knew."

Krzyzewski paused briefly, recounting the moment.

"I can't even put it into words, really," he said. "It's a hell of a thing."

And so the two men met out on the deck, overlooking a beach with the sound of the waves crashing in the distance. Krzyzewski could not be sure that Dean could understand him and Linnea did not know, either. Yet "even in the end stages," she said, she knew that "he could feel the caring."

"Up until the end he could sense that," she said. "And that gave him, I think, comfort, or some peace. So he sensed it. He sensed the caring, and that came across."

Linnea knew what that final meeting between two old rivals meant to her husband, even if he couldn't articulate it. Earlier this week she wondered what it might have meant to Krzyzewski, and she figured she had a good idea from the time he visited her husband that day at the beach, and her experience being by Dean's side through two national championships, hundreds of victories, retirement and then his long goodbye.

"Mike talks about the rivalry and the intensity and the fierceness of the rivalry," she said, "but I think seeing (Dean) so vulnerable would force you to (realize) — no matter how many games you win or what power you perceive you have or how successful you are,

And I love Dean Smith. And I respect the hell out of him.

— MIKE KRZYZEWSKI

that life is finite. That life is fragile.

"Oftentimes we're in denial that you don't have as much time as you thought you did."

It wasn't too long ago, really, that Krzyzewski and Dean Smith were coaching against each other for the final time, or even the first. It wasn't so long ago that Krzyzewski was a young man, trying to prove himself against the old guard; trying, in his own way, to emulate Smith. Now that was all in the past. Krzyzewski, like Smith before him, had come to set a standard.

When Duke's season ends, it'll be the first time since 1960 without Smith or Krzyzewski as a head coach at two schools eight miles apart. For more than 60 years, one or the other remained constants. Back in his office last summer, Krzyzewski again wondered how all of this happened.

His career. The building he was standing in. The peace and friendship he found with Smith toward the end of his life. There was a significance that Krzyzewski's final home game would come against North Carolina, beyond the routine familiarity that every other regular season ends that way, with a home game against the Tar Heels.

"There's a level of security there," he said, "because you're in this penthouse of excellence. But you don't get all of it. You've got to fight like hell for some of it. And then you respect how the others have fought like hell for it."

It took him years of defeats to learn that. It took his earliest Final Fours to earn that kind of respect. Now after all these decades, all these games against UNC that taught him "to fight like hell," he'd reached an endpoint of his own.

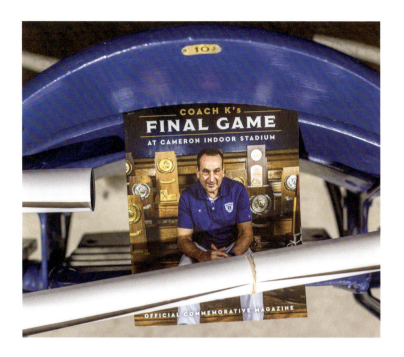

ABOVE: Duke coach Mike Krzyzewski directs his team on defense in the first half, coaching his final game in Cameron Indoor Stadium against North Carolina on March 5, 2022, in Durham, N.C. ROBERT WILLETT / THE NEWS & OBSERVER

ABOVE LEFT: Each seat in Cameron Indoor Stadium had a commemorative poster and program for ticket holders which honors Duke head coach Mike Krzyzewski as he coaches his final home game on March 5, 2022. ROBERT WILLETT / THE NEWS & OBSERVER

LEFT: Duke coach Mike Krzyzewski reacts as he is recognized by Duke's president Vincent Price with five scholarships in the Krzyzewski name, following the Blue Devils' 94-81 loss to North Carolina on March 5, 2022, in Durham, N.C. ROBERT WILLETT / THE NEWS & OBSERVER

After 42 years, Coach K's last home game brings tears, unexpected loss

BY ANDREW CARTER, THE NEWS & OBSERVER• PUBLISHED MARCH 5, 2022

DURHAM, N.C. — By 8:20 Saturday morning, there was already a long line of people, most dressed in royal blue, most carrying love notes written in marker on poster board, stretching from the entrances on either end of Cameron Indoor Stadium. They'd come from all over to be a part of Mike Krzyzewski's final home game at Duke, and even a pregame show that began nine hours before the main event felt like an event, nonetheless — something to witness.

It was early then, the sun still climbing over the pines that line Duke's campus, and Krzyzewski had already arrived for work. He'd parked his black Cadillac Escalade in his usual spot, steps away from the tower where his office resides up on the sixth floor, with an endless view of campus and beyond. He walked into the building alone, a good 45 minutes before any other member of his staff arrived.

The parking lot didn't exist when Krzyzewski became the Blue Devils' head coach in 1980. Neither did the office tower. It came much later, years after he led Duke to the first of its five national championships. Nonetheless, his routine was familiar as ever. He'd begun most mornings for the past 42 years the way he began Saturday, arriving at Duke and walking into work.

And now it was happening for the final time on a game day at Cameron Indoor Stadium. At one point on Saturday, hours before tip-off against North Carolina, Krzyzewski took a moment in his office to look out into the distance, across the rectangular lawn that over the years came to be known as Krzyzewskiville. What he saw stayed with him, even after a 94-81 defeat that will, without question, be remembered among the most stunning and disappointing of his career.

"I was amazed at the number of people in Krzyzewskiville," he said later, after a postgame celebration in his honor that at times looked tortuous for him, given the circumstances. "The atmosphere for the whole day was incredible. Just incredible. And I was hoping, because our guys walked through there and all that, that (it) would help us."

This was not the ending anyone foresaw, or the one that seemed preordained. Krzyzewski often references the Basketball Gods — those invisible forces that might make a team go hot, or cold — and those Gods proved cruel to Duke on Saturday. The Blue Devils held a 7-point lead with a little less than 13 minutes remaining and then appeared to hit a Carolina blue wall.

Duke's lead gradually shrunk and then disappeared all together. In the final moments, the inevitability set in. A hush fell over the

---

OPPOSITE: Duke coach Mike Krzyzewski speaks during a press conference ahead of his final home game against North Carolina on March 3, 2022, in Durham, N.C.
ROBERT WILLETT / THE NEWS & OBSERVER

crowd. Krzyzewski, especially conversational with officials during the first half, and at times as animated as ever, stood still throughout most of the final minutes. The defeat assured, he placed his hands on his hips. He crossed his arms.

He finally took a seat. He didn't stand again, until it ended.

"He was disappointed in how we played, how we finished" said Paolo Banchero, Duke's standout freshman who, along with his teammates, was helpless to slow the Tar Heels' onslaught during the final 10 minutes or so.

Banchero spoke quietly, as if he wasn't quite sure what could be said. Wendell Moore, the Duke junior, wasn't any more illuminating a few feet away.

"We just couldn't get a stop," he said.

In the second half, UNC, at times, made it look easy. Krzyzewski and his coaching staff, meanwhile, felt helpless to offer anything from their vantage point on the far end of the court, opposite the one where the Blue Devils stumbled again and again defensively. Krzyzewski built his program in the 1980s and '90s on tough, menacing defense, but

Duke's defense was "just horrible," he said, in the second half.

There was, perhaps, one surprise. Krzyzewski, known for his hard outer shell, allowed the emotion of the day to overcome him a time or two. He said he hadn't expected to cry. It surprised him when he did in the moments before tip-off.

That was the power of it all. The realization that this was it, in this building. The return of so many former players. The understanding that there'd never be another work day like this one, a morning drive to the office, followed by a shootaround, followed by a game in a building where he'd won 572 times. And so the tears came, more than once early on.

"Then the game started," Krzyzewski said, "and I was crying more about how we were playing."

More games to play

For 42 years, he has had the same job. Day after day. Week after week. Months turning into years, into decades, until it reached an end, of sorts, Saturday.

There will be more games to play. Krzyzewski made sure to offer a reminder of that — first telling the crowd in the moments after the defeat, at the start of a celebration in his honor, that the season was not yet over.

"It's time to move on now," he said about 30 minutes later, in front of a roomful of reporters.

Throughout his final season, Krzyzewski has been adamant about staying in the moment, resisting overtures to go too far back into the past. He resisted the talk of the last of this, or that, but there was no escaping such reflection because it was here: his last home game. The final time he'd make the walk from the Duke locker room and across the court to the home bench, and the final time he'd walk off that court, win or lose.

The atmosphere inside the building, at least for the first 37 or 38 minutes of game time, until the reality set in late, matched that on the outside. For hours, people came to walk around and soak it in. It felt equal parts like an outdoor music festival and an SEC football tailgate, like a celebration and also a little like a somber farewell. Nobody wanted to say goodbye, and then the moment came when Krzyzewski appeared on the court for the first time.

The roar was deafening. Duke recovered from a sloppy start, took a slim lead into halftime and seemed on the verge of pulling away. And then, in a sweltering old gym and amid the most pressure any Blue Devils team had faced in a long time — the burden of winning this particular game, in this particular moment — Duke succumbed.

It wasn't the magnitude of the moment, Banchero and Moore said afterward.

It was more that on this particular night, the Tar Heels were better.

Krzyzewski wondered about the psychology of it all. In a way he and his players had spent much of the past week basking in some kind of anticipated coronation, like a eulogy for the living.

"Basically we're living in a penthouse these last few days," Krzyzewski said, "with room service and everyone saying nice things. And we didn't play hungry today."

A lingering defeat

Before Saturday, he'd endured 75 defeats in this building. The 76th will linger.

It came on his 15,327th day on the job at Duke, one that began like thousands of those other days and ended with Krzyzewski hugging his wife, Mickie, and embracing his 10 grandchildren during a postgame ceremony in his honor.

For most of it — the parts where a video played overhead, or while people spoke — Krzyzewski sat in a chair and looked for all the world like a man who'd have rather been anywhere else but there, listening to people say nice things about him after a defeat against a bitter rival.

"We didn't play well," he told the crowd in an unscripted moment, before turning to the dozens of former players, all dressed in the same white pullovers, who were still standing behind the Duke bench. "And there were times when you didn't, either."

There was a small laugh, a brief moment of levity. Soon, Krzyzewski embraced his family, told his wife and daughters and grandkids that he loved them, even more than basketball, and walked off the court for the final time. So

many things had changed around him over 42 years, in the sport where he'd made his name and outside of it, but Cameron Indoor Stadium looked largely like it did from the day he walked in. Some things would endure.

"I'm glad this is over," he told reporters moments later, though it wasn't as though he hadn't appreciated the celebration of his career and his program. It was, instead, that he desired to get back to it. He'd coached his final home game, yes, but he wasn't done. It was the losses, he said, that offer the greatest lessons.

The tears were gone now. The reality had set in. He'd lost for the final time in the building where he'd won hundreds of times; where he'd built one of the most successful college athletics programs in American sports history. There'd be no opportunity to leave with a better taste, no chance to walk off this court a winner one last time. That opportunity was gone, replaced by the one ahead.

"Let's just coach and see what the hell happens in the tournaments," he said, and not long after that he'd answered his final question and disappeared, back toward his office.

At around 11 p.m., Krzyzewski's Escalade was still in its parking lot. It'd been there for 15 hours by then. The lights were on upstairs in the upper floors of the tower next to Cameron, where workers were cleaning up. The next time Duke played here, it would no longer be Krzyzewski's team — though for now it still was, however long the season might last. A practicing Catholic, Krzyzewski had to be at Mass in about eight hours.

After a defeat that will undoubtedly stay with him, he hadn't yet left work.

Let's just coach and see what the hell happens in the tournaments.

— MIKE KRZYZEWSKI

Coach K's plan for his life after coaching has been decades in the making

BY STEVE WISEMAN, THE NEWS & OBSERVER

There was a morning in October 2021 that Mike Krzyzewski spent the first part of his day talking Duke basketball with reporters at the ACC's Tip Off event in an uptown Charlotte hotel.

Such events had become commonplace for Krzyzewski, who was about to begin his 42nd season coaching the Blue Devils, but instead of discussing strictly basketball like he had for the 41 preseason interviews that preceded this day, the topic of conversation was his impending retirement.

Enough time had passed since he announced in June that 2021–22 would be his final season that the shock of college basketball's all-time winningest coach retiring had worn off. But it was still, four months later, all anyone around the ACC wanted to talk about.

That afternoon, he headed back to Durham and, a little after 4 p.m., sauntered into Durham Academy's Moylan Field to meet up with his wife, Mickie, and other family members.

Game planning and practice review took a back seat as he focused on Emmie Savarino, his 17-year-old granddaughter who was playing in the final home game of her Durham Academy field hockey career.

With that, he transformed from Hall of Fame coach to, as his 10 grandchildren refer to him, Poppy.

"The grandparent thing is part of it," Krzyzewski said of his decision to retire from coaching.

Krzyzewski has since made the full transition out of coaching, handing the program to Jon Scheyer, allowing the 75-year-old to stop devoting countless hours to the game as he has over the last 42 years while turning Duke into one of the nation's elite basketball programs.

"He was at tons of my basketball games when I was a kid," said Jamie Spatola, Krzyzewski's youngest daughter and the one of his three children who took up the sport that has made his name famous. "He's always done that."

But now there will be more time for it, which Krzyzewski is ready to embrace while at the same time promising not to overdo it and funnel his competitive fire through them.

"Well, I won't be a helicopter grandparent, getting on the coach's ass," Krzyzewski said. "But just to show interest."

That goes for no matter what extracurricular activity his grandchildren pick, be it Emmie's field hockey or 11-year-old John David Spatola's ninja warrior competitions or, yes, the basketball that 12-year-old Rem Frasher already plays so well.

"But also if they would be involved in theater or whatever," Krzyzewski said. "You

---

OPPOSITE: Duke head coach Mike Krzyzewski is introduced during Countdown to Craziness at Cameron Indoor Stadium in Durham, N.C., Oct. 15, 2021. ETHAN HYMAN / THE NEWS & OBSERVER

want to show an interest. Not just show an interest, you are. I am interested in them. We are lucky to have 10 grandkids."

The Krzyzewskis keep up even when they can't physically be present. Mickie honed her IT skills finding livestreams allowing her and her husband to watch from home.

So even when Emmie's sister, Carly, plays a volleyball match for Saint Mary's School in Raleigh, her grandparents are watching.

"Sometimes this tech work is a tedious process but they do it," said Debbie Savarino, Carly and Emmie's mother and the oldest Krzyzewski daughter. "Two 75-year-olds figuring out the tech stuff to watch their grands. The best."

The long road to retirement

In many ways over the decades as Krzyzewski's family grew in Durham, he and Mickie have prepared themselves for the time that will arrive next spring, when it's time to step away from coaching.

Their West Cornwallis Road home, just across the Orange County line, abuts Duke Forest. They have a pool, basketball court and bocce ball court.

Lindy Frasher, his middle daughter, lives less than a mile away with her husband, Steve, and their three children. Peter and Debbie Savarino and their family live around 4 miles away. Jamie Spatola, her husband Chris and their three children are 6 miles away.

None live more than 15 minutes away from their parent's home, a fact that Krzyzewski treasures.

"All 10 of my grandchildren are here, in the area," Krzyzewski said. "They come over to swim all the time. So that's been a cool thing."

He paused for a second, realizing how normal it's become for families to spread and scatter all over the country and thus appreciating his situation even more.

"Really? In this day and age?" Krzyzewski said. "That doesn't happen."

He and Mickie have their favorite vacation spots, like Las Vegas where they escaped last April between the end of the basketball season and his retirement plan announcement. Or heading to Napa Valley, California, where they headline an annual V Foundation for Cancer Research fundraiser.

He'll take time to enjoy more of those trips, which he could only sample while coaching Division I basketball at Army West Point and Duke continuously since 1975.

Staying put on campus

That said, he will have plenty to do at Duke after coaching. He's under contract to work as an ambassador for the school, a position in which Duke president Vince Price said Krzyzewski will be "an advisor and counselor to me and to my colleagues across campus and beyond."

"The thing about retiring," Krzyzewski said, "we are involved with so many things. I'm going to stay in this office. We're on the sixth floor. We have this (Duke basketball) Legacy Fund that we're running. I'll be involved, just like I am now, in so many aspects of the university. Probably a little bit more, although we are pretty involved."

An adjunct professor at Duke's Fuqua School of Business for the last two decades, he'll continue to work with students there in addition to speaking to students around the campus in other disciplines.

"We are going to be a part of Duke's continuing journey, like President Price said, for as long as we are around," Krzyzewski said.

For years he's given speeches around the country through the Washington Speakers Bureau, where his booking fees are more than $70,000.

Out of the spotlight, he makes calls or prepares hand-written notes to people fighting cancer or other life-threatening diseases, usually complete strangers.

He'll continue to host his SiriusXM radio show, which airs weekly during the fall and winter. It's called Basketball and Beyond with Coach K and, perhaps, it will involve more of the beyond topics starting next year.

"In the future, they've talked about maybe doing something different," Krzyzewski said. "I've really enjoyed that show. I've gotten to meet so many people. And people want to be on. So that's good."

Helping shape college basketball, NCAA

But basketball, the sport that took him

> "
> "My cup will runneth over by the end of this year with maybe college basketball. And I've had a damn big cup and I'm grateful for it, really.
>
> — MIKE KRZYZEWSKI

from his inner-city Chicago neighborhood to West Point for what he calls the education that changed his life, to now being among the most accomplished, famous and wealthy people in his profession, will still be part of his life in one way or another.

"I'll probably get involved in some way with basketball," he said, "but maybe at the NBA level, if I could, with consulting or something. You never know."

Jamie Spatola has one particular task for her dad to tackle.

"Part of me wants him to help figure out college basketball," Spatola said. "In some ways, it feels like it would take someone with that universal authority to be able to have an impact."

Krzyzewski doesn't hide his frustration with how the NCAA manages basketball. He's often said the sport needs a czar while quickly saying he doesn't want the job.

"People have been saying I've been vying to run the NCAA," he said. "No way. No way. I've tried to do it behind the scenes for 40 years. For 40 years."

College football runs its own playoff system separate from the NCAA. That leaves March Madness, the men's and women's basketball tournaments, as the main source of income for the organization.

This month, a virtual constitutional convention will take place aimed at massively overhauling the NCAA's structure. The NCAA Board of Governors will consider proposals from the constitutional committee in December and voting on a new structure could take place in January.

Krzyzewski's problem is with all these meetings, where changes and improvements are discussed behind closed doors and too often no progress is made. That's allowed a system to perpetuate that, at its best, hasn't always been fair to all people and, at its worst, has been more sinister, Krzyzewski said.

"Always some nameless committee where you can say anything you want and you are not held accountable," Krzyzewski said. "There are different agendas in that meeting and I don't want to get into it. But all I know is our sport is primarily black. A lot of stoppages along the years have been because of that. I believe that. And by the way, a lot of African American coaches believe that."

Because Krzyzewski said such things while coaching Duke, the natural conclusion many drew is he was doing it to somehow help the Blue Devils win more games.

In December 2020, before COVID-19 vaccines were available and cases and deaths were spiking, Krzyzewski raised the idea of pausing the season for a few weeks until vaccines could be administered. Alabama coach Nate Oats suggested it was only because Duke had already lost home games to Michigan State and Illinois.

"Do you think if Coach K hadn't lost the two non-conference games at home he'd still be saying that?" Oats said.

Oats later apologized. Still, maybe when Krzyzewski is done coaching, accusations of him being self-serving might disappear.

But it shouldn't matter, because as his family and others closest to him say, it has nothing to do with wins and losses.

"This is real," Jamie Spatola said. "Whatever you think of the value of sport in society — perhaps it shouldn't hold the esteem that it does — it sure is a place to teach young people and to remind ourselves of certain fundamental values of how to treat people and work together. He means that. He's not just trying to win games."

Of course, he has won games — 1,170 of them, more than anyone who's ever coached college basketball.

Basketball will always be a part of what he's doing.

"My aunts and mom have literally grown up in basketball, just like me," said Michael Savarino, Krzyzewski's second-oldest grandson who is in his third season playing for his grandfather with the Blue Devils.

"Obviously, completely different childhoods but their childhoods being completely surrounded by basketball. You eat, sleep and breathe it because of coach."

Coach K's treasured family time

But even while building a coaching career in basketball with few, if any, peers, Krzyzewski has always been close to his family — maybe closer than they realized.

"He doesn't have a ton of one-on-one time with each of my children and that's one thing I hope for more in retirement," Jamie Spatola said. "But when we are together, he does observe them individually. I'll find myself being 'Oh, my dad really doesn't know my kids well.' But he will pull me to the side and say something so poignant about one of my kids I'll be like, 'Oh my gosh how does he know that?' I know that's his gift. He sees people. He sees people's gifts. He sees people's insecurities, people's pain. And he often knows what to do and he's always willing to take the time to do it."

With his final game behind him, the basketball coaching part of Krzyzewski's life is complete.

"It's good," Krzyzewski said. "I'm happy. I hope you can sense I'm happy. Really looking forward to this year but I'm also looking forward to the future. My cup will runneth over by the end of this year with maybe college basketball. And I've had a damn big cup and I'm grateful for it, really. You are lucky."

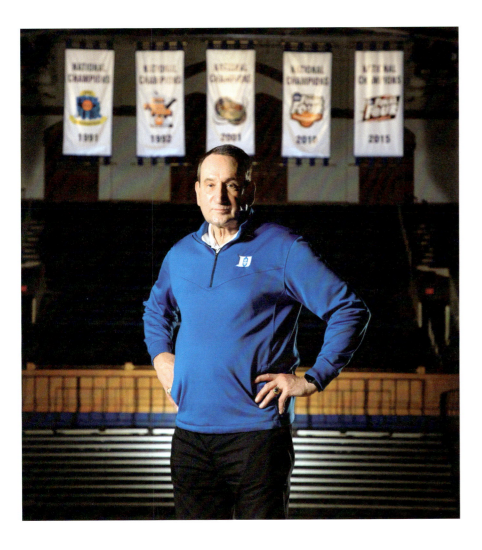

LEFT: Duke coach Mike Krzyzewski poses for a portrait in Cameron Indoor Stadium in Durham, N.C., Nov. 2, 2021. ETHAN HYMAN / THE NEWS & OBSERVER

A dog named Blue

BY LUKE DECOCK, THE NEWS & OBSERVER

After Duke's plane returned to RDU from New York in the wee hours of the morning, Nov. 3, 2021, Mike and Mickie Krzyzewski headed back home in the dark, and when they turned up the circular driveway of their house, that face wasn't there waiting.

The dining room window next to the front door is empty. The familiar yellow face, ecstatic at the coach's return, wasn't there for the first time in more than a decade.

Krzyzewski went through his final season as Duke's head coach without his constant companion of the last 12 1/2 years, a yellow Labrador named Blue who watched more film with the coach than any of his assistant coaches.

Took more walks than any of them, too.

"He was my guy," Krzyzewski said. "When I came home, the walks, I work outside a lot, watching tape — he's there. I miss him."

Blue died in Krzyzewski's arms in the summer of 2021, a week after being diagnosed with lung cancer. It's a measure of Krzyzewski's grief that he brought it up, unprompted, during an August media briefing.

He had sporadically mentioned Blue over the years — "I don't have a doghouse. I have a dog. His name is Blue," Krzyzewski said in 2013 — but never like this. It was an unburdening, a rare moment of uncontainable private grief displayed publicly for a perpetual companion.

"Always. And a good one," Krzyzewski said later. "And also, not just as a guy, but also at my age you don't just have somebody new to fool around with. He was good. A great dog with the kids. People. He was just a good guy. Just a real good guy."

Anyone with a dog — any pet, really — has their own relationship with it, but there's something different with coaches who have dogs: A working companion during all the late hours, a walking partner during constitutionals to blow off steam or clear one's head, an unfailingly friendly face after the hardest losses, or when even when the die-hardest fans and wealthiest boosters have lost faith.

If you need a friend in coaching (or many other cutthroat pursuits), get a dog, the saying goes.

Krzyzewski has had three.

The first two — a black Lab named Defense and a chocolate Lab named Cameron — were family dogs, companions for his daughters as much as a coach who didn't have dogs growing up and had to learn to love them.

"Defense was my dad's first pet," Krzyzewski's daughter Jamie Spatola told The N&O's Steve Wiseman, a phrasing that could potentially apply to basketball as well.

Blue, who was born just before Krzyzewski won his fourth national title in 2010, was different. The girls were long out of the house. When Krzyzewski got home from work or the road, Blue was always there, waiting impatiently for his walk.

"As soon as I came in," Krzyzewski said. "Even though I'm talking to Mickie, he was like, 'Let's go. Let's go.'"

When you've been somewhere as long as Krzyzewski has been at Duke, there are fundamentals that become constants, a routine that becomes a comfort as much as it is a means to an end. That's changing for Krzyzewski now. He's already off the recruiting trail, almost but not quite fully disengaged from that process. While fully invested in the Xs and Os of this Duke season, his interactions with successor Jon Scheyer will necessarily increase as part of the transition.

These are small but jarring changes for someone as set in their (successful) ways as Krzyzewski has been. And yet none of them will be as personally disruptive as this final season spent without the furry, floppy companion who was by Krzyzewski's side when no one was watching.

Blue's role wasn't filled during Krzyzewski's final season. "We haven't recruited anyone to replace him," Krzyzewski joked in August, because Mickie wants to travel with the team during this farewell season and it wouldn't be fair to a new dog to spend that much time alone.

Selecting a replacement for the irreplaceable Blue will be one of Krzyzewski's first and more important post-retirement tasks. Even if he was unsure, his family may insist upon it.

"That man needs, he needs a dog," Spatola said. "He needs a dog."

OPPOSITE: Duke basketball coach Mike Krzyzewski walks with his dog Blue, circa 2011. Blue died in Krzyzewski's arms during the summer of 2021. CHUCK LIDDY / THE NEWS & OBSERVER

He was good. A great dog
with the kids. People.
He was just a good guy.
Just a real good guy.

— MIKE KRZYZEWSKI

Coach K's 13th Final Four berth at Duke is among his sweetest

BY ANDREW CARTER, THE NEWS & OBSERVER • PUBLISHED MARCH 27, 2022

SAN FRANCISCO — Mickie Krzyzewski stood near the corner of the court and waited. The final minutes turned into the final seconds, the anticipation building. It was real now, one part of the storybook dream turning into reality. This is a walk she'd made many times, from the first row of the seats at an NCAA tournament regional final to the edge of the court and then onto it to celebrate with her husband, another trip to the Final Four secure.

Now it was different, though. She knew this would be the final time, just like everybody knew this would be the final time. Mike Krzyzewski is retiring whenever Duke's NCAA tournament journey ends, and for a while it looked like it might end last week against Michigan State, in Greenville, S.C., just like for a while it looked like it might end here at the Chase Center on Thursday night, against Texas Tech.

Instead, here were the Krzyzewskis, Mike and Mickie, embracing on Saturday night in a far corner of the court near the Duke bench. After two agonizing victories, the kind that might age a younger coach and even tested Krzyzewski's mettle, the Blue Devils made it look comparatively easy during their 78-69 victory against Arkansas in the West Regional final.

The horn sounded and the celebration began and Mickie waited patiently for her husband to find her in the aftermath. When he did the cameramen gathered all around them. Their family was lined up nearby, their daughters and their grandchildren, and a few of their longtime friends, too. A crew of workers hustled past, carrying parts of the makeshift stage they were assembling for the victory ceremony. Blue and white confetti had fallen from the ceiling. Duke had done it.

"I can't explain it," Mike Krzyzewski said several minutes later, while some of his granddaughters bent to the court and gathered pieces of that confetti and tossed them up over their heads, creating a blue and white paper shower. "I'm a grandfather, and

I've lived through my daughters. (Now) I'm living through my grandchildren."

Krzyzewski first experienced this kind of moment back in 1986, when his hair was jet black and when his future as a college basketball coach seemed much less certain than it soon became. Some Duke supporters had wanted him fired before that breakthrough. In '86, when Krzyzewski first led Duke to the Final Four, he was a much younger man — not even 40.

He and Mickie were a young couple, at least much younger than they are now, after more than 50 years of marriage. His trips to the Final Four became milestones to mark the years, and perhaps there was a part of him on Saturday night that could look back and see some of those past celebrations, his little girls becoming young women and then mothers themselves; his family expanding, some of the grandkids growing up before his eyes.

That was part of why his voice cracked a bit Saturday night, during the celebration on the

---

OPPOSITE: Duke head coach Mike Krzyzewski hands the net to his players after cutting it down after Duke's 78-69 victory over Arkansas in the NCAA tournament West Regional finals at the Chase Center in San Francisco, March 26, 2022. ETHAN HYMAN / THE NEWS & OBSERVER

THE FINAL SEASON • 123

court. He's a 75-year-old man now — an "old man," he called himself at one point during Duke's postgame press conference — and he's traveling this road for the last time. That the journey will end in New Orleans, in his 13th Final Four, is all Krzyzewski could've hoped for when he announced his retirement early last June; indeed, it's the stuff of Hollywood or boyhood dreams, to go out like this.

Yet what makes this regional championship even grander, beyond the fact that Krzyzewski is now at most eight days away from coaching his final game, is how the Blue Devils won it. It wasn't that long ago when Duke was thought to be too young and too inconsistent. Wasn't that long ago when the rap against the Blue Devils was their toughness, and whether they possessed the kind of fortitude to survive this tournament.

They were a consistent top-10 team throughout the season, yes, but they melted down during that humiliating defeat against North Carolina in Krzyzewski's final home game. In the ACC tournament championship game defeat against Virginia Tech, Duke allowed the Hokies to look a little like the Golden State Warriors, and there in Brooklyn, too, Duke lacked much fight. And besides, before Thursday Duke had never won a game out West in the NCAA tournament in Krzyzewski's 42-year career.

And so yes, he said on the court after his team had won the one regional he never had, this is different. It's the first time since 1994 that Duke has advanced to the Final Four without being a No. 1 seed. It's the first time ever that Duke has made a Final Four with this kind of roster composition, with a team so reliant on freshmen and without a senior starter.

"This isn't that four-year team," Krzyzewski said, "or even (2015), where you have Amile (Jefferson), Quinn (Cook), Matt Jones — they're really young."

Now Jefferson is a member of Krzyzewski's staff and Jones was there Saturday night, among the masses in the maw of the post-game celebration. Mike Dunleavy, a member of Duke's 2001 national championship team, was there, too, while Grant Hill, among the leaders of the 1991 and '92 title teams, worked the West Regional with Jim Nantz and the rest of CBS' lead broadcasting crew.

Krzyzewski's farewell season has been the dominant story in college basketball over the past several months and everything surrounding that story — the drama and the exposure and the attention — has only increased in March. It has made for a cauldron of pressure and yet for once, after stress-test victories against Michigan State and Texas Tech, Duke allowed itself a chance to exhale in the final minutes against Arkansas.

The folks behind the Duke bench, Krzyzewski's family and friends and one white-haired man in the first row who goes by Pucci, could feel the impending victory throughout much of the second half. They could feel it especially when the lead grew to 18 with 6 1/2 minutes remaining, and soon enough Mickie Krzyzewski was making her way to the corner of the court to greet her husband.

"The most amazing moment," said John Pucci, a longtime Las Vegas casino executive formerly at the Wynn and now with Caesar's Palace, who insisted people only knew him by the one name, his last, like Madonna or Prince. "Like Zorro."

Pucci and Krzyzewski have become close friends over the past 20 years — close enough that Pucci was right behind the Duke bench Thursday and Saturday nights; close enough to hear Krzyzewski pleading with his team to muster some defensive stops against Texas Tech, and close enough to watch Krzyzewski breathe easier with the Blue Devils in control against Arkansas.

"We've become so close," Pucci said. "But tonight was an amazing moment because he's retiring, and everybody thinks when you're going to retire you're done." He's not done. We're going on. We're going to carry the flag out in New Orleans, too. ... He's going to go out with a sixth ring. That's what I think."

It is becoming a more and more realistic thought, though that was for another night to decide. On this one, Krzyzewski embraced the people closest to him and stopped to share a few quick thoughts while all around him his players and their families soaked this in.

Duke is certainly Duke, as former Virginia coach Pete Gillen once said, creating a meme before anyone knew what a meme was. And yet the Blue Devils celebrated Saturday night not as though they represented one of the

> "
> ## I'm so proud of you guys, and happy for you. You've crossed the bridge, man.
>
> — MIKE KRZYZEWSKI TO HIS TEAM

most successful programs in the history of the sport, but as if they weren't sure this moment would arrive.

A good number of these Blue Devils had never played in an NCAA tournament game before this team's first, which had come eight days earlier, in Greenville, when Duke's direction seemed much less certain. And in college, at least, no member of this Duke team had ever climbed a ladder to cut down a net following a championship. Paolo Banchero, the Blue Devils' freshman forward, had wanted to climb such a ladder after a high school championship. He'd been left somber that it didn't happen.

He shared the story Saturday night, wearing a hat that said FINAL FOUR on it.

"My mom won a state championship as a coach, and she got to go up on the ladder and cut the net, and I remember her swinging the net around and (saying) I always wanted to do that," Banchero said. "Then I won state in high school, and they lowered the hoop to cut the net. They didn't bring the ladder, and so it kind of ruined the moment a little bit."

When he climbed the ladder Saturday night, Banchero said, he locked eyes with his mom. He said he told her, "Make sure you get this on video, and get a picture."

Listening to the story to Banchero's right was Krzyzewski, beaming like a father.

"That was good," he said. "That's really good."

Moments earlier Krzyzewski had turned to his players when they'd arrived in the interview room and, unprompted, told them that they'd been "terrific," which is one of Krzyzewski's go-to words when he's pleased, along with "my guys" — as in, "proud of my

LEFT: Duke's Wendell Moore Jr. (0) heads to slam in two during Duke's 78-61 victory over Cal State Fullerton in the first round of the NCAA tournament at Bon Secours Wellness Arena in Greenville, S.C., March 18, 2022. ETHAN HYMAN / THE NEWS & OBSERVER

guys." He hadn't had an opportunity to use any of those during the first two Saturdays in March, after defeats against Carolina and Virginia Tech, but he could use them now.

"I'm so proud of you guys, and happy for you," Krzyzewski said. "You've crossed the bridge, man."

For the next several minutes, Krzyzewski did his best to keep himself and his players in this moment. It was as though he didn't want to think about anything except having just won the West. He deflected one question about the prospect of meeting North Carolina, again, in the Final Four.

Krzyzewski swatted away another question, directed at Banchero, about whether the Blue Devils felt confident they could send their retiring coach out a national champion for the sixth time. That was when Krzyzewski referred to his age, saying, "They've won a (conference) regular-season championship and they've won the western regional championship. They did that.

"They did it for us, and enough about doing it for the old man here," he said.

It was true, in a way: Krzyzewski has aged. The hair isn't quite as black. The step isn't as spry. He limps when he walks, especially when he's out of sight, away from the bench and in the bowels of an arena before or after a game. Sometimes it looks as though he's in pain, like the work isn't comfortable anymore. Not that he showed it, much, in the heat of the moment.

Next to him his players were trying to put this all into words, with Jeremy Roach, the sophomore point guard, acknowledging the pain of last season and how "we came back hungry," and Wendell Moore Jr., a junior forward who is a captain and the most experienced of Duke's starters, saying, "You come to Duke looking to get to moments like this."

Moore and Roach, like their teammates, were carrying souvenirs — the pieces of the net they'd cut down — and earlier, on the court, Krzyzewski had done the honors on the final strand. He'd just spent a few minutes around a crowd of reporters, a couple of his granddaughters playing in front of him, when he said, "I'm going to go cut down the net," and with that he made his way slowly to the ladder and climbed it while someone handed him some scissors.

Soon he was waving that net around, as jubilant as when he'd first done it a decades ago, and it had been a long time, seven years, since he'd had the occasion to climb a ladder during an NCAA tournament. If Duke had lost before now, Krzyzewski's career would've ended with its longest Final Four drought. Instead, it continues on.

A good 45 minutes after the final buzzer, some of Duke's players and their parents were still on the court, taking everything in. They posed for pictures. They embraced each other. The blue and white confetti was everywhere, still. It was almost like nobody wanted to leave, as if they wanted to remain in this moment forever.

But the journey wasn't yet finished. Duke would celebrate throughout the night and return home to North Carolina, if only briefly.

Krzyzewski's final March would stretch into April. New Orleans awaited.

RIGHT: Duke's Jeremy Roach (3) drives past Cal State Fullerton's Vincent Lee (13) during the first half of Duke's game against Cal State Fullerton in the first round of the NCAA tournament at Bon Secours Wellness Arena in Greenville, S.C., March 18, 2022. ETHAN HYMAN / THE NEWS & OBSERVER

ABOVE: Duke's Paolo Banchero (5) drives to the basket past Michigan State's Marcus Bingham Jr. (30) during the second half of Duke's 85-76 victory over Michigan State in the second round of the NCAA tournament at Bon Secours Wellness Arena in Greenville, S.C., March 20, 2022. ETHAN HYMAN / THE NEWS & OBSERVER

ABOVE LEFT: Duke head coach Mike Krzyzewski talks with his team during the first half of Duke's game against Michigan State in the second round of the NCAA tournament at Bon Secours Wellness Arena in Greenville, S.C., March 20, 2022. ETHAN HYMAN / THE NEWS & OBSERVER

LEFT: Duke's Jeremy Roach (3) shoots as Michigan State's Max Christie (5) defends during Duke's 85-76 victory over Michigan State in the second round of the NCAA tournament at Bon Secours Wellness Arena in Greenville, S.C., March 20, 2022. ETHAN HYMAN / THE NEWS & OBSERVER

ABOVE: Duke's Wendell Moore Jr. (0) goes for the ball with Texas Tech's Terrence Shannon Jr. (1) during the first half of Duke's game against Texas Tech in the Sweet 16 round of the NCAA tournament at the Chase Center in San Francisco, March 24, 2022. ETHAN HYMAN / THE NEWS & OBSERVER

ABOVE RIGHT: Duke head coach Mike Krzyzewski argues a call during the first half of Duke's game against Texas Tech in the Sweet 16 round of the NCAA tournament at the Chase Center in San Francisco, March 24, 2022. ETHAN HYMAN / THE NEWS & OBSERVER

OPPOSITE: Duke's Jeremy Roach (3) drives to the basket as Texas Tech's Kevin McCullar (15) defends during Duke's 78-73 victory over Texas Tech in the Sweet 16 round of the NCAA tournament at the Chase Center in San Francisco, March 24, 2022. ETHAN HYMAN / THE NEWS & OBSERVER

RIGHT: Duke's Paolo Banchero (5) celebrates with Jeremy Roach (3) after Roach made a shot late in the second half of Duke's 78-73 victory over Texas Tech in the Sweet 16 round of the NCAA tournament at the Chase Center in San Francisco, March 24, 2022. ETHAN HYMAN / THE NEWS & OBSERVER

ABOVE: Duke's Paolo Banchero (5) drives as Texas Tech's Terrence Shannon Jr. (1) defends during the second half of Duke's 78-73 victory over Texas Tech in the Sweet 16 round of the NCAA tournament at the Chase Center in San Francisco, March 24, 2022. ETHAN HYMAN / THE NEWS & OBSERVER

ABOVE RIGHT: Duke's Jeremy Roach (3) passes out of the pressure by Texas Tech's Kevin McCullar (15) and Terrence Shannon Jr. (1) during Duke's 78-73 victory over Texas Tech in the Sweet 16 round of the NCAA tournament at the Chase Center in San Francisco, March 24, 2022. ETHAN HYMAN / THE NEWS & OBSERVER

OPPOSITE: Duke head coach Mike Krzyzewski and his wife, Mickie, embrace after Duke's 78-73 victory over Texas Tech in the Sweet 16 round of the NCAA tournament at the Chase Center in San Francisco, March 24, 2022. ETHAN HYMAN / THE NEWS & OBSERVER

RIGHT: Duke's Mark Williams (15), Paolo Banchero (5), Wendell Moore Jr. (0) and AJ Griffin (21) head back towards their basket during the second half of Duke's 78-73 victory over Texas Tech in the Sweet 16 round of the NCAA tournament at the Chase Center in San Francisco, March 24, 2022. ETHAN HYMAN / THE NEWS & OBSERVER

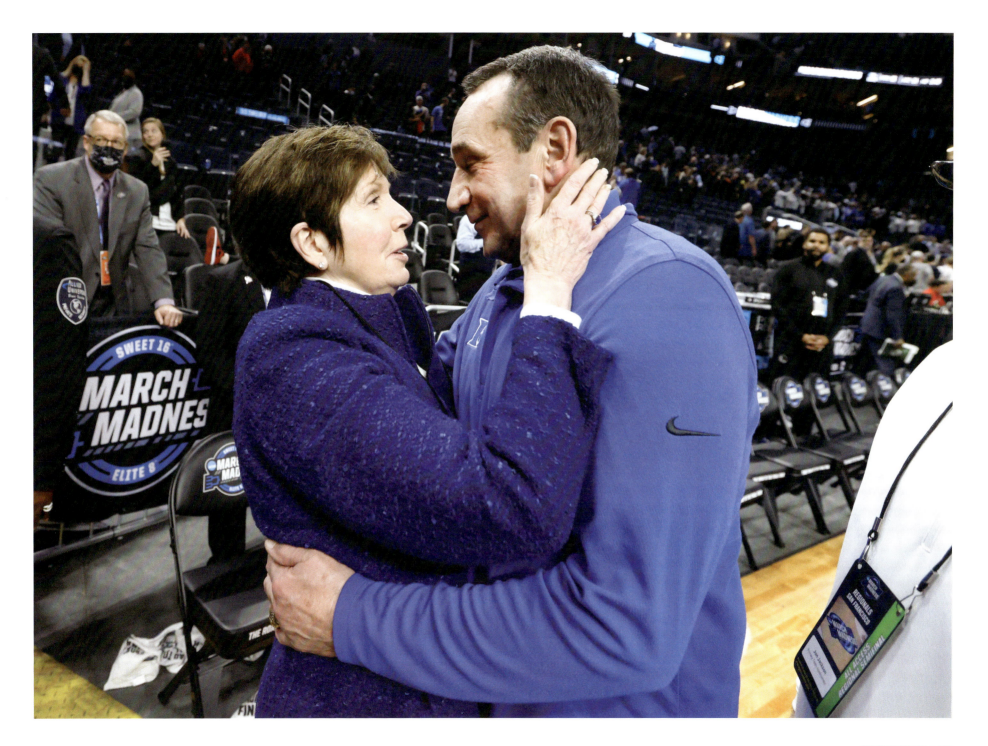

ABOVE: Duke's AJ Griffin (21), Wendell Moore Jr. (0) and Trevor Keels (1) huddle after a timeout during the second half of Duke's 78-69 victory over Arkansas in the NCAA tournament West Regional finals at the Chase Center in San Francisco, March 26, 2022. ETHAN HYMAN / THE NEWS & OBSERVER

RIGHT: Duke's Wendell Moore Jr. (0) is called for the foul as he drives into Arkansas' Jaylin Williams (10) during Duke's 78-69 victory over Arkansas in the NCAA tournament West Regional finals at the Chase Center in San Francisco, March 26, 2022. ETHAN HYMAN / THE NEWS & OBSERVER

LEFT: Duke's AJ Griffin (21) celebrates after cutting the net after Duke's 78-69 victory over Arkansas in the NCAA tournament West Regional finals at the Chase Center in San Francisco, March 26, 2022. ETHAN HYMAN / THE NEWS & OBSERVER

OPPOSITE: The Duke Blue Devils celebrate with the West Regional Trophy after Duke's 78-69 victory over Arkansas in the NCAA tournament West Regional finals at the Chase Center in San Francisco, March 26, 2022. ETHAN HYMAN / THE NEWS & OBSERVER

BELOW LEFT: Duke's Paolo Banchero celebrates after Duke's 78-69 victory over Arkansas in the NCAA tournament West Regional finals at the Chase Center in San Francisco, March 26, 2022. ETHAN HYMAN / THE NEWS & OBSERVER

Holding hands under a fluorescent sunset, Coach K at peace on other side of Duke career

BY ANDREW CARTER, THE NEWS & OBSERVER • PUBLISHED APRIL 3, 2022

NEW ORLEANS — It was late Saturday night now, almost midnight local time, when Mike Krzyzewski emerged from the Duke locker room for the final time as the Blue Devils' head coach. He'd held that job for 42 years and 16 days and until recently, at the start of his last NCAA tournament, he could always take comfort that there'd be another walk like this, another game.

Now it was over. His players had cleared out and their tears had told Krzyzewski that he'd done his job with this team, no matter the 81-77 defeat Duke suffered against North Carolina in an unforgettable national semifinal at the Superdome. Most of his assistants had left, too, by the time Krzyzewski walked out, slowly and painfully, just a few steps behind his wife, Mickie.

For weeks now they'd endured this final March, and early April, it turned out, together. It became a familiar scene: the Duke bus pulling up hours before tipoff in Brooklyn or Greenville, S.C., or San Francisco and the Krzyzewskis stepping off together, Mike and Mickie, and walking hand-in-hand into another arena before another game.

For weeks they'd walked out the same way, holding hands, and triumphantly. Each NCAA tournament victory — against Cal State Fullerton and Michigan State in Greenville; against Texas Tech and Arkansas last week in the West Regional — moved Krzyzewski one game closer to his sixth national championship and the ultimate storybook ending in his final season.

Saturday brought an ending, but not that ending; not the one of dreams or fairytales or the one that little by little began to look ever more realistic the longer Duke's postseason journey lasted. By the end of it, Krzyzewski wore the look of a man who had expended all of his energy. He sounded hoarse when he met with reporters. His eyes suggested he might've shed some tears, too.

It was fitting, perhaps, that his final game came against North Carolina, the old nemesis from just down the road and one that somehow, as a No. 8 seed, found its way to New Orleans and the Final Four. In his earliest years at Duke, Krzyzewski built his program in the shadow of what Dean Smith had long established at UNC; and then the two schools spent more than 30 years going back and forth and back again, both playing their part in what arguably became sport's greatest rivalry.

The Tar Heels and Blue Devils played each other for the 258th time on Saturday night, and none of the previous 257 had come in an NCAA tournament game, much less one in the Final Four. The 40 minutes of game time they shared in the Superdome became a microcosm of the rivalry: One team taking

---

OPPOSITE: Duke associate head coach Jon Scheyer talks with head coach Mike Krzyzewski during the second half of UNC's 81-77 victory over Duke in the Final Four at Caesars Superdome in New Orleans, April 2, 2022. ETHAN HYMAN / THE NEWS & OBSERVER

control only for the other to take it back; big shots on one end met with big shots on the other; the margin so thin, the outcome was in doubt until the end.

By then, in the final minute, there was little for Krzyzewski to do other than watch from his seat atop a little stool in front of his team's bench. The stool sat atop the raised court inside the Superdome, giving Krzyzewski the appearance of a king on a throne, only now the fate of his coaching career was largely out of his hands and belonged to his players. For about two weeks, he'd gushed about how far his youngest team had come, how quickly it had grown up, but the sort of magic that Duke found late in victories against Michigan State and Texas Tech now became elusive.

Krzyzewski watched from the stool, waiting and hoping for the kind of moment that never arrived. At times he sat upright, arms folded and staring ahead. In other moments he leaned forward, his arms on his knees. Throughout his final season, he'd resisted the constant overtures to look back into the past, to contextualize his 42 seasons at Duke, or look too far into the future and to consider what the ending might be like and what retirement would bring.

He was focused on the now, he'd say. Sometimes he'd reference the training he'd received back at West Point, more than 50 years ago now, when he was a cadet in the U.S. Military Academy. He learned there to block out anything else but the mission. But now, in the final moments of Saturday night, focusing on the now meant focusing on the fact that it was all ending. This game. This long chapter of his life.

He turned his eyes upward, toward the clock, and watched the seconds of his coaching career run out. When he rose from the stool it looked as though he'd also played for 40 minutes, like UNC starters Caleb Love and Leaky Black, and indeed after most timeouts Saturday night a manager handed Krzyzewski a small cup of water that he'd quickly sip until it was time for another.

The ending brought pandemonium, for Carolina. The Tar Heels celebrated on the court, their players and coaches and some of their family members dancing and jumping and elating in this moment in front of the UNC cheering section on one end of the Superdome. UNC was onto the national championship game for the first time since 2017, and it'd been expected back then, when the Tar Heels were on a season-long mission to avenge the at-the-buzzer defeat they'd suffered in the 2016 championship game, against Villanova.

On the other end of the court, meanwhile, Duke's managers cleared the Blue Devils' bench. Krzyzewski lingered only briefly, to shake hands with UNC's players after he'd done the same with the Tar Heels' coaching staff, and then he disappeared into a long tunnel in one corner of the arena and made a right toward the locker room. He remained inside for a long time and later he said that he appreciated what he saw, for what he saw was proof that his team had wanted this as badly as he did.

"I've said my entire career — or when I knew what the hell I was doing — that I wanted my seasons to end where my team was either crying tears of joy or tears of sorrow because then you knew that they gave everything," Krzyzewski said. "And I had a locker room filled with guys who were crying. And it's a beautiful sight. It's not the sight that I would want. I'd want the other. But it's a sight that I really respect and makes me understand just how good this group was."

Krzyzewski was speaking then during his final press conference, and the room was full. Down in front of him, photographers jockeyed for position to document the moment while reporters tried to get him to describe his own emotions at the ending — "It's not about me, especially right now," he said once, before offering versions of the same in other moments — while members of his family filled a large section of seats to Krzyzewski's far left.

There was Mickie, resting her head on the shoulder of one of her grandsons. And there were Krzyzewski's daughters, their eyes watery. And there were all the grandchildren, ranging from small kids to young adults. For their entire lives, they'd known nothing other than a world in which their grandfather coached at Duke, just as anyone alive 41 or younger had known the same. And now it was over, two nights earlier than Krzyzewski and his family and his players had envisioned.

Try as he might to resist the overtures for broader perspective as it related to his thoughts and emotions, Krzyzewski soon enough found himself referencing Theodore Roosevelt's "Man in the Arena" speech. Perhaps it was something he'd learned at West Point a long time ago or maybe he'd picked it up somewhere along the way, but now it fit, the reference to a 112-year-old speech about the power of competition itself, regardless of the outcome.

"I'll be fine," Krzyzewski said then. "I've been blessed to be in the arena. And when you're in the arena, you're either going to come out feeling great or you're going to feel agony, but you always will feel great about being in the arena.

"And I'm sure that that's the thing, when I'll look back, that I'll miss. I won't be in the arena anymore. But, damn, I was in the arena for a long time. And these kids made my last time in the arena an amazing one."

Krzyzewski's ride into a superimposed sunset

When his press conference ended, Krzyzewski lingered for a while with his family, out of sight, in a holding area beyond the view of reporters or anyone else. On the other side of a curtain, more than a dozen photographers surrounded the golf cart that waited to give Krzyzewski and his wife a ride back to the locker room on the other side of the Superdome. His arrival, at last, was met with a chorus of shutter clicks, and after Krzyzewski led Mickie onto the back of the cart and sat down next to her he smiled and thought of a bit of dry humor:

"Maybe you all can superimpose a sunset," he said under the yellow glow of old industrial lighting, as he began to ride off, and he offered a short wave. Moments later, he

> "
>
> ## I'll be fine. I've been blessed to be in the arena.
>
> — MIKE KRZYZEWSKI

LEFT: Duke head coach Mike Krzyzewski watches during Duke's open practice at the Caesars Superdome in New Orleans, April 1, 2022. ETHAN HYMAN / THE NEWS & OBSERVER

thanked those who'd gathered to document the moment.

To understand this moment, though, and Krzyzewski's career ending, was to understand how it all began. He became Duke's head coach on March 18, 1980, during the Jimmy Carter administration. He was relatively unknown in the profession, so much so that he spent part of his introductory press conference pronouncing and spelling his name for the local media. He was young then, 33, and looked a little nervous to be on that stage, taking over an ACC program.

He entered a neighborhood, among UNC and N.C. State, in which Duke was the least-accomplished of its rivals. Both the Tar Heels and Wolfpack had won national championships; Duke had not. In those days, it was the UNC-State rivalry that gripped North Carolina, and while Duke was not an afterthought, it was a long way from becoming what it became.

When Krzyzewski got the job, he and Mickie bought a modest home north of downtown Durham and that in itself was a small miracle, Krzyzewski said before the season began,

because "we had no money." It was 1980 and the economy was faltering and after living in Army housing while he coached there, Krzyzewski had no house to sell, no equity to help him get his start in North Carolina. He could still remember the interest rate for his first mortgage in Durham: 18 percent, he said, and as he looked back in time — a rare moment of deeper reflection amid all the others in which he has attempted to avoid it — Krzyzewski began to become thankful.

"Crazy," he said. "It's just — I've been so damn lucky. I mean, something's

good happening."

In that moment he was sitting in his expansive sixth-floor office, atop a basketball tower that Duke built in 1999, seven years after the second of Krzyzewski's five national championships. He was surrounded by all the history of the past 42 years: photographs documenting those titles; moments of jubilation on the court with family members and his players; mementos from one of the greatest coaching careers in American sports history.

And yet amid all of it, Krzyzewski acknowledged there was still a void that would never

RIGHT: Duke's Paolo Banchero (5) dunks against North Carolina's Leaky Black (1) in the second half. ROBERT WILLETT / THE NEWS & OBSERVER

really be filled. That even after winning more games than anyone in his profession had ever won he still felt a constant need to prove himself, over and over again. Maybe he owed that part of himself to his insistence that he never look too far back, for better or worse, or maybe he owed it to his humble origins in Chicago, where his Polish roots and meager means did not make for an easy childhood.

"I think I've always been trying to prove myself," Krzyzewski said then, before the season, and in a way that was part of what drove him throughout the past several months, the question of whether he could

guide his youngest team to the level it eventually reached. The neverending quest to prove himself has roots, too, in another part of Krzyzewski that is perhaps at odds with all the stay-in-the-moment philosophizing he'd done during much of this season, and especially recently.

"He never forgets anything," Mike Cragg, one of Krzyzewski's closest friends, said recently. Cragg spent more than three decades working in the Duke athletic department and came to know Krzyzewski well before Cragg became the athletic director at St. John's in 2018. Now Cragg could tell no shortage of

stories about what motivated Krzyzewski, what stuck with him.

"The thing about Coach K is that nobody's going to outwork him. Nobody's going to, in anything. I'm not just talking about basketball, but just that he is relentless in the pursuit of excellence."

Cragg then was talking specifically about how the tribulations of the early-to-mid-80s shaped Krzyzewski and molded him into what he became. The Blue Devils finished 10-17 in Krzyzewski's second season and 11-17 the next, and that one ended with a blowout defeat against Virginia in the ACC

tournament, a loss that had a good number of Duke supporters calling for Krzyzewski to be fired. In a different time, perhaps one more like today, governed by instant gratification and social media takes, Krzyzewski might not have lasted another season. Tom Butters, the Duke athletic director at the time, kept the faith in his hire, though, and rewarded Krzyzewski with a contract extension in 1984, when it became clear he had Duke headed in the right direction.

Even so, it's easy to forget the broader context of that moment. Dean Smith had just led the Tar Heels to a national championship in 1982, and UNC was clearly the dominant program in the neighborhood if not the country. Jim Valvano and N.C. State followed with the 1983 national championship, leaving State and UNC with two national titles apiece and Duke with none.

Krzyzewski's national breakthrough came in 1986 with the first of his 13 Final Fours. It was a team with a core of seniors, including Johnny Dawkins and Mark Alarie, who'd been freshmen during the 11-win humiliation of 1983. Suddenly Duke was off. The Blue Devils reached the Final Four again in 1988 and '89 and '90, only to fall short, before they broke through in '91 with the first of their consecutive national championships.

Three other championships followed, in 2001 and 2010 and 2015, and Krzyzewski became the kind of omnipresent figure, more than four decades in the same job, that might never again exist at his level of college basketball. The game is what he lived, whether it was at Duke or with the U.S. National Team, and it was the pursuit of winning — "of excellence," as Cragg put it — that drove him as much this season, at 75, as it did when he was 33 and in his first year at Duke.

It was a pursuit that could rub people wrong. Like his college coach and one-time mentor, Bob Knight, Krzyzewski became a polarizing figure. He was royalty at Duke, and to the legions of Blue Devils fans throughout the country. To others, he became easy to disdain, in part because of all the winning but also because of how he won, with an intensity that could border on maniacal.

Krzyzewski developed a reputation for berating officials. For showering them with a storm of F-bombs in moments of frustration. JJ Redick, who left Duke as the ACC's all-time leading scorer, recalled during a recent podcast a moment when he returned to Duke and sat behind the bench for a game. As Redick told it, Krzyzewski gathered his team during a timeout, looked at each one of his players and said:

"I hate your (expletive) faces."

It was the sort of comment meant to motivate, though Krzyzewski's detractors would surely view it differently. To those who loved to hate him, Krzyzewski became the New York Yankees and Darth Vader rolled into one, a man who might as well have entered the arena to the tune of "The Imperial March." And yet part of Krzyzewski's legacy, too, is his founding of the Emily K Center, named in honor of his mother, and the smaller moments of human connection that went unnoticed.

Cragg thought about the notebook Krzyzewski always carries with him, the one with the Duke logo on the cover. As always, Krzyzewski carried that notebook everywhere with him throughout his final postseason, from the ACC tournament in Brooklyn to the West Regional in San Francisco to here in New Orleans, where he had it tucked under his arm during the Blue Devils' shootaround on Friday.

"His notebook always has notes and letters and emails, and he's always working, always taking notes," Cragg said, describing the notebook where Krzyzewski keeps correspondence with people who've contacted him for advice or guidance or hope. "And so the world has no idea. No idea how many people he has touched, called, that are coming from just simple letters to him, asking for help, or introducing themselves. You know, 'My child has cancer' — I mean, nobody has any idea.

"And he never did it for any other reason than he cares about people."

A peaceful finish for Krzyzewski

Almost a month ago now, after consecutive Saturdays that ended with defeats against North Carolina, in Krzyzewski's final home game, and Virginia Tech, in the ACC tournament championship game, this sort of run to the Final Four did not seem possible for Duke, or all that likely. Then the Blue Devils underwent a metamorphosis that had them believing in the fairytale ending before it gave way to the tears of defeat late Saturday night.

When Krzyzewski emerged from his team's locker room the first time after his final loss, for his postgame press conference, he walked into a scene of juxtaposition. A few of North Carolina's players were just a few feet away, conducting interviews after their victory. Krzyzewski made his way to the podium where, when he arrived, a few of his own players sat to his left, their pain evident. Each of them described what this ride had been like, being on Krzyzewski's final team and having been a part of final March, and April.

"For me, it's been everything," said Wendell Moore Jr. "... It was a dream of ours to come here. Coach delivered on every promise he gave us, and even more. ... He does it with his heart. He does everything with his heart. He loves each and every one of us dearly. And we all love him.

"So we can do nothing but thank him for everything he's done for us."

Said Trevor Keels: "Coach K always has been there for me. ... And I think all of us left it out there and played with joy. We had fun out there. We came up short, but we for sure had fun out there."

And Paolo Banchero, who likely will be among the first players selected in the next NBA Draft: "He was so committed to us all year. Never made it about him. And you're just proud that we were able to go out and fight, be in a fight, with Coach every game."

Soon enough the press conference, like the game before it, was over. The final one of Krzyzewski's coaching career. Another moment that'd come and gone, and suddenly there was a final date on the other side of the dash representing the length of Krzyzewski's time at Duke as the Blue Devils' head coach: March 18, 1980–April 2, 2022.

He'd won 1,202 games, including the 73 victories during his first five seasons at Army. He'd won five national championships and 15 ACC tournament championships. Now, though, after a lifetime of attempting to prove himself, there was nothing more to prove. At least not on this stage.

He and Mickie rode back to the locker room together and remained inside for 15 or 20 minutes before walking out again, this time for good. It was quieter now, the cameras that had been lurking before were now all gone. A cart waited to give Krzyzewski and his wife a ride back to the bus, which waited on the other side of the Superdome.

Mickie climbed on the back first, covering herself in a Duke blue shawl. Krzyzewski, walking with a limp and as if he was in pain, sat down next to her and moved in close. For a moment she rested her head against his shoulder and chest, and he put an arm around her and kissed the top of her head. The locker room grew more distant, little by little, and so did the court.

They rode like that together, comforting each other, and soon the cart rounded a curve in the hall and disappeared toward the bus. Mickie boarded first and then Krzyzewski. And for the first time in more than 50 years, since before his days as a college player, or even in high school, there was no next game to anticipate. The final one had come and gone. Krzyzewski looked tired but strangely content, even after one of the more difficult losses of his career. He appeared ready for the end, as if he'd already made peace with it.

He took his seat near the front of the bus, surrounded by his team but alone with his thoughts. A few minutes before midnight the bus began to pull away. Slowly, the arena itself became more distant behind Krzyzewski, and he rode off not into the sunset but into the dark of night after a draining defeat. Already it was almost a new day, the first of his retirement.

RIGHT: Duke's Trevor Keels (1) misses a 3-point attempt with :04 seconds to play against North Carolina, securing the Tar Heels' 81-77 victory. ROBERT WILLETT / THE NEWS & OBSERVER

OPPOSITE: Duke head coach Mike Krzyzewski and his wife Mickie smile after saying goodbye to the media as they leave the post-game press conference after North Carolina's 81-77 victory over Duke. ETHAN HYMAN / THE NEWS & OBSERVER

A year-by-year look at Coach K's career

SEASON	SCHOOL	CONF	W	L	FINAL AP RANKING	NOTES
1975–76	Army	Ind	11	14		
1976–77	Army	Ind	20	8		
1977–78	Army	Ind	19	9		
1978–79	Army	Ind	14	11		
1979–80	Army	ECAC	9	17		
1980–81	Duke	ACC	17	13		
1981–82	Duke	ACC	10	17		
1982–83	Duke	ACC	11	17		
1983–84	Duke	ACC	24	10	14	NCAA tournament
1984–85	Duke	ACC	23	8	10	NCAA tournament
1985–86	Duke	ACC	37	3	1	ACC season and tournament champion; Final Four
1986–87	Duke	ACC	24	9	17	NCAA tournament
1987–88	Duke	ACC	28	7	5	ACC tournament championship; Final Four
1988–89	Duke	ACC	28	8	9	Final Four
1989–90	Duke	ACC	29	9	15	Final Four
1990–91	Duke	ACC	32	7	6	ACC season championship; NCAA championship
1991–92	Duke	ACC	34	2	1	ACC season and tournament champion; NCAA championship
1992–93	Duke	ACC	24	8	10	NCAA tournament
1993–94	Duke	ACC	28	6	6	ACC season championship; Final Four
1994–95	Duke	ACC	9	3		
1995–96	Duke	ACC	18	13		NCAA tournament
1996–97	Duke	ACC	24	9	8	ACC season championship; NCAA tournament
1997–98	Duke	ACC	32	4	3	ACC season championship; NCAA tournament
1998–99	Duke	ACC	37	2	1	ACC season and tournament champion; Final Four
1999–00	Duke	ACC	29	5	1	ACC season and tournament champion; NCAA tournament
2000–01	Duke	ACC	35	4	1	ACC season and tournament champion; NCAA championship
2001–02	Duke	ACC	31	4	1	ACC tournament championship; NCAA tournament
2002–03	Duke	ACC	26	7	7	ACC tournament championship; NCAA tournament
2003–04	Duke	ACC	31	6	6	ACC season championship; Final Four
2004–05	Duke	ACC	27	6	3	ACC tournament championship; NCAA tournament
2005–06	Duke	ACC	32	4	1	ACC season and tournament champion; NCAA tournament
2006–07	Duke	ACC	22	11		NCAA tournament
2007–08	Duke	ACC	28	6	9	NCAA tournament
2008–09	Duke	ACC	30	7	6	ACC tournament championship; NCAA tournament
2009–10	Duke	ACC	35	5	3	Reg. Season Champion; Conf. Tournament Champion; NCAA championship
2010–11	Duke	ACC	32	5	3	Conf. Tournament Champion; NCAA tournament
2011–12	Duke	ACC	27	7	8	NCAA tournament
2012–13	Duke	ACC	30	6	6	NCAA tournament
2013–14	Duke	ACC	26	9	8	NCAA tournament
2014–15	Duke	ACC	35	4	4	NCAA championship
2015–16	Duke	ACC	25	11	19	NCAA tournament
2016–17	Duke	ACC	28	9	7	ACC tournament championship; NCAA tournament
2017–18	Duke	ACC	29	8	9	NCAA tournament
2018–19	Duke	ACC	32	6	1	ACC tournament championship; NCAA tournament
2019–20	Duke	ACC	25	6	11	
2020–21	Duke	ACC	13	11		
2021–22	Duke	ACC	32	7		Reg. Season Champion; Final Four
Career	**Duke**		1129	309		
	Army		64	59		
	Overall		1202	368		